RESOLVING SOCIAL CONFLICTS

SELECTED PAPERS ON GROUP DYNAMICS

By Kurt Lewin

Late Director, Research Center for Group Dynamics
Massachusetts Institute of Technology

Edited by
GERTRUD WEISS LEWIN

Foreword by
GORDON W. ALLPORT

A CONDOR BOOK
SOUVENIR PRESS (EDUCATIONAL & ACADEMIC) LTD

A/301. 1

CONTENTS

FOREWORD
by Gordon W. Allport
PROFESSOR OF PSYCHOLOGY, HARVARD UNIVERSITY

IN THE course of his highly productive life Kurt Lewin never wrote a textbook. Monographs and articles were his preferred means of expression. It was through them and through his personal influence upon students and colleagues that he wrought a not inconsiderable revolution in the scientific study of man in society.

But students need textbooks. Articles and monographs are inaccessible, expensive, non-consecutive. Up to now the student wishing to understand Lewin's system of thought has turned to *A Dynamic Theory of Personality*, a collection of papers published in 1935, or to *Principles of Topological Psychology*, an exposition of key concepts at an advanced level, printed in 1936. Both of these volumes were issued before Lewin had fairly begun his notable studies in the field of social science. Now, fortunately, we have the present collection of papers to serve as a convenient sourcebook in Lewinian social psychology.

Although written at various times between the years 1935 and 1946, the thirteen chapters here arranged for publication provide a logical progression of thought. They dovetail so well that they seem almost to have been written intentionally for publication in a single volume. The unifying theme is unmistakable: the group to which an individual belongs is the ground for his perceptions, his feelings, and his actions. Most psychologists are so preoccupied with the salient features of the individual's mental life that they are prone to forget it is the ground of the social group that gives to the individual his figured character. Just as the bed of a stream shapes the direction and tempo of the flow of water, so does the group determine the current of an individual's life. This interdependence of the ground and the figured flow is inescapable, intimate, dynamic, but it is also elusive.

Some authors, tackling this elusive relationship, have spoken loosely about "group influence on the individual," about "cultural determinism," or the "group mind." Some have over-simplified the relationship in their exaggerated claim that "personality is merely the subjective side of culture." Others have solved the problem by slicing the individual into segments: those segments regarded as determined by social factors are said to form "the basic personality structure," and this structure is thought to apply to all members of a group; the remaining segments are regarded as biologically determined or as "idiosyncratic." But all such attempted solutions fail, either because they beg the question or because they put artificial cleavages where none in fact exist.

Lewin's outstanding contribution is his demonstration that the interdependence of the individual and the group can be studied in better balance if we employ certain new concepts. Although the present volume contains primarily papers having a concrete, case-anchored character, still each shows with clarity how fruitful these new concepts are for understanding the phenomenon in question. Lewin's concepts are arresting because they serve equally well in depicting concrete situations, and in the task of making scientific generalizations. As Mrs. Lewin points out in her Preface, her husband was intent upon erecting a firm bridge between the concrete and the abstract, between social action and social theory. The papers in the present series are best read from this dual point of view. They have a vivid and appealing quality about them because the problems they treat are of unmistakable importance and of interest to all of us. Yet at the same time the exposition weaves ceaselessly back and forth between data and theory, between cases and concepts.

The student may find it helpful to note that Lewin's explanatory concepts are, broadly speaking, of three types. Many of them are adaptations of geometry, or more precisely of topology, a branch of geometry that treats spacial relationships without regard to quantitative measurement. Examples are *space of free movement, life space, region.* The second class of concepts is anchored in the dynamic psychology of the individual (e.g., *need, aspiration level, satiation*). These latter concepts for the most part refer to *systems of tension* within the person himself. Whenever Lewin feels it necessary to speak simultaneously both of these tension systems within the individual and of the pressures emanating from the surrounding field he introduces a third type of concept, such as *field forces* (motives clearly depending upon group pressures), *barriers* (obstacles to individual action owing to group restraints), or *locomotion* (changing of the individual's position with reference to the group). In reality, of course, these three aspects of his thought are not separable. All of his concepts, whatever root-metaphor they employ, comprise a single well-integrated system. Besides these three classes of conceptual tools Lewin employs others whose nature is virtually self-explanatory. Among these we may include: *group atmosphere, levels of reality, time perspective, group decision, we-feeling.* The reader will readily fit these into the total framework of his theory.

Because of the internal consistency of Lewin's system of thought —which for convenience is usually labelled *field theory*—the reader should find little difficulty in learning how to handle the many special concepts that compose the theory as a whole. At the same time it is not necessary to accept the total system in order to benefit from its brilliant insights or to employ advantageously its incisive analytical tools. Some psychologists today who are resistant to certain of Lewin's striking formulations accept others as standard household implements in psychological work. Among the widely accepted concepts are barrier, detour, level of aspiration, central regions of personality, rigidity, satiation, group atmosphere, group decision, action research.

Lewin's methods, no less than his theory, have a pioneer character. Better than any other investigator he has succeeded in adapting experimentation—the preferred method of scientific inquiry—to the complex problems of group life. His ingenuity is striking. Problems that might seem utterly inaccessible to experimentation have yielded to his attack. A decade ago social scientists were invigorated by his demonstration that the elusive subject of political atmosphere could be recast into an experimental design. He boldly created an authoritarian and a democratic group structure for eleven-year-olds and carefully recorded the consequences.

In another connection he asked himself what happens to organized and to unorganized groups under conditions of panic, and found the answer experimentally. He asked: how may overbearing, anxiety-ridden foremen be efficiently retrained so as to improve the social relations, and therewith the production, in a factory? Social scientists were startled by his audacious experiments, and not infrequently criticized them. Yet he never wavered in his conviction, stated at the beginning of Chapter 5 of the present volume: "I am persuaded that it is possible to undertake experiments in sociology which have as much right to be called scientific experiments as those in physics and chemistry."

Before undertaking to reduce a problem of group conflict to a crucial experiment, he spent much time contemplating it in its raw state. Many of the chapters in the present volume are not in fact based upon experimentation but upon his keen and sustained observation of the factors involved in the conflict situation in question. Had time and energy permitted he would, I feel certain, have eventually reduced many more of the phenomena he discusses to experimental study.

In the first chapter—one of the most brilliant in the book—he boldly tackles the problem of comparative national psychology. How do the social grounds in Germany and in America differ, so that children reared in these countries develop appreciably different types of personality? This essay introduces with marked clarity some of the key concepts of field theory, particularly those having to do with the person as a differentiated region marked by surface as well as by deeper layers of organization.

The next three chapters expand the theme, with special refer ence to the problem of democratic re-education. If there are features in a national character that are inimical to the peace of the world, the remedy for the situation lies in altering the political and cultural climate within which the hostile character develops. To make the Germans more democratic, for example, requires an alteration in leadership and in values. For unless the inclusive group structure is altered, individuals cannot basically be changed.

To Lewin the crucial determinant of group atmosphere lies in leadership. A successful resolution of social conflicts requires in nearly all instances the activity of trained, democratic leaders. Nor is such leadership a mere matter of utilizing a few fancy tricks to make people feel good: a democratic leader is not simply a clever persuader. The democratic process is complex, and it is necessary to train both leaders and group members to play their respective roles within it. Even Americans, for all their essential familiarity with democracy, need continually to practice and improve their group activities.

There is a striking kinship between the work of Kurt Lewin and the work of John Dewey. Both agree that democracy must be learned anew in each generation, and that it is a far more difficult form of social structure to attain and to maintain than is autocracy. Both see the intimate dependence of democracy upon social science. Without knowledge of, and obedience to, the laws of human nature in group settings, democracy cannot succeed. And without freedom for research and theory as provided only in a democratic environment social science will surely fail. Dewey, we might say, is the outstanding philosophical exponent of democracy, Lewin its outstanding psychological exponent. More clearly than anyone else has he shown us in concrete, operational terms what it means to be a democratic leader, and to create a democratic group structure.

Part II deals further with this matter. The meaning of democratic relationships is discussed in connection with the problems of boys' clubs, in connection with marriage (a particularly brilliant analysis), in connection with morale both in national groups and in industrial situations. In all face-to-face conflicts we learn that the way in which the individual perceives and interprets the social situation is decisive. His perceptions, objectively viewed, may not (and often do not) correspond to social reality. But cognitive structure must always be studied, so too the individual's perspective in

time. Hope or despair, tenacity or vacillation, clarity or obscurity
in reference to the future, contribute essential qualities to the
psychological situation that exists, and must be taken into account
in seeking remedies. The interesting industrial case study in
Chapter 8 focuses upon these matters, and shows how the application of scientific considerations successfully resolved an acute conflict in personal relations within a factory.

Part III, though it deals with a narrower range of problems—
group prejudice and tension—actually contains two distinct levels
of exposition. Chapter 9, written in 1935, is the earliest of the
papers gathered in the present volume. It speaks of the psychological problems confronting any minority group whose space of
free movement is restricted by discrimination, by barriers of caste
and prejudice. While most members of the majority group can
enjoy multiple memberships in several groups and move freely and
without conflict among them, the Negro, the Jew, the Oriental,
and often the Catholic and other "alien," does not know whether
he has a space of free movement or not. His uncertainty has psychological consequences: often he is restless, often he attacks the
barriers raised against him, especially if he feels that his aggressive efforts may be successful. The psychological situation of a
minority group member is not unlike that of an adolescent who
is never quite sure whether he is dwelling in the world of childhood or of adulthood. It is not surprising that some of the responses of minority group members are very like those of
adolescents. Though written only a short time after the author came
to America, and during the period when he was profoundly concerned with the persecutions in Nazi Germany, this chapter has
about it a classic quality of detachment. With deep penetration
it sets forth the psychological dilemma of minority groups of all
types, in all lands, in all periods of history.

By contrast we note how Chapter 13, written eleven years later,
seems caught in the maelstrom of "action research," with few
clearly marked conclusions. It is significant, I think, that this final
paper in the series is perhaps the least decisive, for at the time of
his death Lewin was still widening the program of his research

and was still in the process of reducing his rich hypotheses to experimental designs. Since the writing of his first paper on prejudice, America had fought the war, had endured dangerous race riots at home, and had become deeply conscious of the problems created by group hostilities. Money had become available for basic research. Lewin inevitably was drawn into this new and vital area of investigation. The type of problem that intrigued him most was the "change experiment." Remedial efforts, he insisted, should be introduced into a community prepared to study the results of its own social action. His program as ever was boldly conceived. The process of retraining attitudes, he knew, requires that participating groups be led to examine their goals and their presuppositions, that members be led to take the roles of other people in the course of the experimental sessions, that they learn to become detached and objective in examining the foundations of their own biases. Chapter 13 outlines his change experiments, but is not in any sense a final report. Before this vital work reached the stage of completion Lewin died, in February 1947. Others, we hope, will succeed in carrying forward his program so that social science may soon learn how to serve effectively the social conscience.

The remaining Chapters, 10-12, form a trilogy of a somewhat special order. Though they make further application of the concepts of life space, marginal membership, and social ground, they are addressed primarily to the Jewish minority. Their purpose is to provide members of this group principles to guide their own conduct in a period of stress. The reader feels both the hard realism and the note of compassion that enter into Lewin's judgments. A Jewish child, he believes, should not be shielded from the situation created by his group membership. It is not safe to assume that the discrimination he will encounter in later life constitutes merely so many hard knocks that he can adjust to when the time comes. The social ground of an individual's life is too important a matter to be left to chance developments. Like a foster child, the Jewish child needs to know from an early age that his conditions of security are in some respects unlike those of an average child. To be clear about one's memberships is the only way for child or for adult to avoid the ravages of anxiety, self-hate, and debilitating resentment. Although Lewin does not in these chapters directly plead the case for Zionism, he makes it clear that a Jewish homeland is a psychological necessity. In no other way can the ambiguous position of the Jews in the world at large find a structured solution.

The contents of this volume are so well selected and so adroitly arranged that it provides an excellent introduction to Lewin's system of thought. To be sure the selection has a social emphasis, and some of the concepts central to his system are not here fully developed. To understand field theory completely the reader will wish to refer also to Lewin's other writings. Yet this volume succeeds in conveying his conviction that theories to be worth their salt must be tested in action, and his conviction that the social ground of mental life must be considered in virtually every psychological act. It contains a full measure of that social realism, of that originality and power, that make Kurt Lewin's life work an important landmark in the scientific study of man in society.

PREFACE

THIS is the first of two volumes of collected writings by Kurt Lewin which are intended to bring together for convenient reading a number of papers he published during the fifteen years he lived in the United States. During this period his scientific interests centered more and more upon problems of social psychology and group dynamics. These two volumes are intended to give a balanced survey of his work, interests, and aims in the study of society, rather than to provide a complete collection of his writings.

While the second volume will present the more theoretical papers, this first collection contains a discussion of a number of practical issues such as those involved in cultural differences and the possibility of re-education, in conflicts in small face-to-face groups such as the family or workers in a factory, or in the special problems of minority groups. The analysis of the nature and causes of social conflicts and the search for techniques capable of preventing or resolving them recur through these papers.

In a certain broad sense the topic of this volume may be called "applied psychology." Kurt Lewin was so constantly and predominantly preoccupied with the task of advancing the conceptual representation of the social-psychological world, and at the same time he was so filled with the urgent desire to make use of his theoretical insight for the building of a better world, that it is difficult to decide which of these two sources of motivation flowed with greater energy or vigor. In an early paper,[1] not published here, in which he laid out the framework for the experimental studies done under his guidance in Germany, he describes the way

[1] Kurt Lewin, *Vorsatz, Wille und Bedürfnis,* Berlin: Julius Springer, (1926).

in which, to his mind, theory and reality have to be linked. He compares the task to the building of a bridge across the gorge separating theory from the full reality of the "individual case." The research worker can achieve this only if, as a result of a "constant intense tension," he can keep both theory and reality fully within his field of vision.

Reading this program for his life's work now, more than twenty years later, with its repeated picture of the bridge to be built, I recall the intense joy, almost ecstasy, that my husband used to feel when he drove his car across the great American bridges, across the Hudson River, across San Francisco Bay. He never tired of admiring these achievements of engineering skill. No doubt he conceived of his particular field of research as equally capable of joining what seemed such widely separated stretches of territory. The connection of theory and the profoundly disturbing social issues of our reality especially led him to experience this intense, persistent "tension."

From the very beginning of his scientific work he had sought to apply his theoretical findings to a number of practical fields, to methods of teaching, to work with problem children, to "psychological satiation" of textile workers. Later the advent of Hitler, the experience of the quick change of a whole society under the totalitarian power field, the impressions connected with living and working in the United States, the possibility of comparing corresponding situations in equivalent social settings, and last but not least his deep personal involvement as a liberal and as a Jew— all this necessarily increased the urge and the tension towards the application of his findings as a social psychologist, as it widened his theoretical outlook in the social field. The Research Center for Group Dynamics which he established at the Massachusetts Institute of Technology was conceived and planned by him as a laboratory to develop just this combination of research and action.

The unifying thread in the papers presented here is, thus, the consistent search for the laws and dynamics of human behavior from a definite theoretical point of view. In assembling what originally had been prepared for varied audiences or groups of readers, we were confronted with the problem of how to handle certain repetitions. The same derivation or the same instance is used in several texts, but any effort to eliminate all duplication would have meant interrupting the trend of thought, breaking a whole into fragments. We felt this would destroy too much and that the otherwise condensed style permitted a certain amount of repetition. We should like the reader to accept them as he would themes in a piece of music which reappear in different contexts and with ever new variations. While in some of these papers there are allusions to events now past, the basic underlying problems have not in the meanwhile been solved. Indeed the happenings of recent years have only confirmed the correctness of earlier diagnosis and prediction. An understanding of the dynamic forces analyzed here is today as essential and indispensable as ever.

We are indebted to the publishers of the original papers for permission to reprint them here. In order to give the reader a better understanding of the social events taking place when each paper was written, the year of publication is given following each chapter title. More specific reference to the date and place of original publication may be cited here:

"Psycho-Sociological Problems of a Minority Group." *Character and Personality*, (1935), III, pp. 175-187.

"Some Social-Psychological Differences Between the United States and Germany." *Character and Personality*, (1936), IV, pp. 265-293.

"Time Perspective and Morale." *Civilian Morale*, Second Yearbook of the Society for the Psychological Study of Social Issues, ed. Goodwin Watson, Chapter IV. Boston: Houghton Mifflin, (1942), Henry Holt and Company, present publishers.

"Self-Hatred Among Jews." *Contemporary Jewish Record*, (1941), IV, pp. 219-232.

"Experiments in Social Space." *Harvard Educational Review*, (1939), IX, pp. 21-32.

"When Facing Danger." *Jewish Frontier,* September, (1939).

"Cultural Reconstruction." *Journal of Abnormal and Social Psychology,* (1943), XXXVIII, pp. 166-173.

"Conduct, Knowledge, and Acceptance of New Values." *Journal of Social Issues,* (1945), I, pp. 53-63. [Written together with Paul Grabbe].

"Action Research and Minority Problems." *Journal of Social Issues,* (1946), II, pp. 34-46.

"Bringing up the Jewish Child." *Menorah Journal,* (1940), XXVIII, pp. 29-45.

"The Background of Conflict in Marriage." *Modern Marriage,* ed. Moses Jung, Chapter IV. New York: F. S. Crofts, (1940).

"The Solution of a Chronic Conflict in Industry." *Proceedings of Second Brief Psychotherapy Council,* Chicago: Institute for Psychoanalysis, (1944), pp. 36-46.

"The Special Case of Germany." *Public Opinion Quarterly,* Winter, (1943), pp. 555-566.

I am greatly indebted to Dr. Dorwin Cartwright for his competent advice and help with the planning and editing of this collection. Mr. Simon N. Herman and Mr. Benjamin Willerman have given useful advice and criticism. I wish also to thank Miss Dorothy Southmayd for her invaluable and conscientious assistance with all the details of preparing the manuscript.

GERTRUD WEISS LEWIN

Newtonville, Massachusetts
January 2, 1948

PART I. PROBLEMS OF CHANGING CULTURE

I

SOME SOCIAL-PSYCHOLOGICAL DIFFERENCES BETWEEN THE UNITED STATES AND GERMANY

(1936)

EDUCATION is in itself a social process involving sometimes small groups like the mother and child, sometimes larger groups like a school class or the community of a summer camp. Education tends to develop certain types of behavior, certain kinds of attitudes in the children or other persons with whom it deals. The kind of behavior and the attitude it tries to develop, and the means it uses, are not merely determined by abstract philosophy or scientifically developed methods, but are essentially a result of the *sociological* properties of the group in which this education occurs. In considering the effect of the social group on the educational system, one generally thinks of the ideals, principles, and attitudes which are common within this group. Indeed, ideals and principles play an important part in education. But one will have to distinguish the ideals and principles which are "officially" recognized from those rules which in reality dominate the events in this social group. Education depends on the real state and character of the social group in which it occurs.

The educational processes, even within a small educational unit like the family, depend to a high degree on the spirit of the larger social body in which the persons are living. Any change in the political, economic, or social structure of this larger group, like the nation, deeply affects not only the organization of education, but its whole spirit and technique as well.

Of course the educational system in every nation varies greatly within different families and schools. Nevertheless, there exists a *general cultural atmosphere* which is the "background" for all special situations. In sociology, as in psychology, the state and event in any region depend upon the whole of the situation of which this region is a part. The general atmosphere has, therefore, a direct bearing upon the education within any sociological unit. The degree of this influence depends mainly upon the degree to which the educational unit in question (the particular family or school) is dynamically separated from the larger enclosing region.

In recent decades we have had striking examples of the high degree to which a changing distribution of political power has changed both the aim and practice of education. Those who have had the opportunity to observe closely enough the behavior of schoolteachers (for instance, in Germany between 1917 and 1933, especially in the period 1931-1933) could easily see how even small changes in the general political situation affected, almost from day to day, not only the ideals which they taught, but also the educational methods which they employed (such as the type and frequency of punishment, the amount of drill, and the degree of freedom and independence in learning.) Times of political change show very impressively the high degree to which education, in nearly all of its aspects, depends upon the social structure of the group. *It seems to be easier for society to change education than for education to change society.*

METHODOLOGICAL CONSIDERATIONS

As obvious as this influence of the sociological situation on education is, and as sensitively as education reacts even to the smallest changes in society, it is nevertheless difficult to determine just what these changes are and to find concepts which express them adequately. The influence which the change in a social situation has on education can not be characterized adequately by describing the changing of programs and organizations, because these facts do not sufficiently determine the dynamic factors of the educational situation, that is, those factors which constitute the influence of education on the behavior, the personality, and the ideals of the growing child. The degree of pressure under which the child stands is generally more important than any particular educational measure or single educational act.

One may argue that such general characteristics as "freedom," "authority," and "social atmosphere" are too vague and too delicate to be grasped through any really strict concepts. Yet one will have to realize that such general terms are not only commonly used in characterizing a particular education, but are, in fact, most important dynamic characteristics of any social-psychological situation. To some extent "human nature" is everywhere the same and certain social characteristics are alike in all capitalistic states within the so-called "western culture."

OBSERVED DIFFERENCES
THE SPACE OF FREE MOVEMENT

If one approaches the description of a situation from a dynamic point of view (that is, from a point of view which should finally allow prediction), one has to understand the situation as a totality of possible events or actions. Every change in its social position, like promotion from one grade to the next, or becoming friends with a group of children, or change in wealth of one's family, means that certain things, persons, or activities are made available or cease to be available. One may speak here of the *space of free movement* and its boundaries. By movements, we have to understand not only bodily locomotions but, above all, social and mental "locomotions." These three kinds of locomotion are somewhat different, but all three are to be recognized in psychology and sociology as real events.

The space of free movement of a person or a social group can be represented as a topological region encircled by other regions that are not accessible. Mainly two factors prohibit the accessibility of regions. One is the *lack of ability*, for instance, lack of skill or intelligence. The other is *social prohibition* or any kind of taboo which stands as a dynamic "barrier" between the person and his goal. The child may be able to grasp an apple, but the mother may have forbidden him to do so.

For the educational situation, the extent of free movement is a most fundamental characteristic. In an institution, for instance, it is generally more restricted than in a family. If the progressive movements of the last twenty-five years in education have emphasized the idea of freedom, this has meant chiefly two things: the recognition of the child's own needs and will, and the avoidance of too many restrictions. Such tendencies should increase the child's space of free movement.

It is not easy to compare the actual space of free movement of the average child in the United States and in pre-Hitler Germany. To compare, for instance, the general instructions for teachers does not lead very far, because the same words have different meanings in different countries; and the gap between the ideals which the educational procedure pretends to follow and the actual procedure is often remarkable. A more reliable symptom seems to be the technical procedures the teachers use, such as the frequency of intervention, the conditions under which they intervene, whether they talk commonly with loud or low voices, etc.

A second difficulty for the comparison is the fact that one can find in both countries families and institutions which grant very little freedom to the children, while the children in other families and institutions are quite free. Furthermore, there are differences between the educational institutions in different parts of the United States and within Germany, and differences between different social classes. In comparing the two countries one should, therefore, as far as possible, refer to children of similar classes and to institutions of equivalent status and function in both countries. Since my experience in the United States concerns mostly people of the middle class, I will refer mainly to this group. Nevertheless, somewhat similar differences may be found between other social strata in both countries.

To one who comes from Germany, the degree of freedom and independence of children and adolescents in the United States is very impressive. Especially the lack of servility of the young child toward adults or of the student toward his professor is striking. The adults, too, treat the child much more on an equal footing, whereas in Germany it seems to be the natural right of the adult to rule and the duty of the child to obey. The natural relation of adult and child is in the United States not considered that of a superior (*Herr*) to a subordinate (*Untergebener*) but that of two individuals with the same right in principle. The parents seem to treat the children with more respect. Generally they will be careful, when requesting the child to bring some object, to ask them in a polite way. They will let the child feel that he is doing them a favor in a situation in which the German parent is much more likely to give short orders. It is more common in the United States to hear a parent thank the child after such action. The parent may even do so after he has had to apply considerable pressure in order to make the child comply, whereas the same situation in Germany would probably lead to "the next time you should do it right away." In Germany the adult will tend to keep the child in a state of submission, while the American may want to put the child back on an equal footing as soon as possible.

The American will often say to a child, "If I were you, I would do that and that," in a situation in which a German might say, "You have to do that immediately." Of course such difference may be merely a matter of differences in the style of language. For on the whole, the American is more apt to use polite language. But such differences of style are themselves significant (see below). At any rate there seems to be a real difference in the degree of respect for the right and the will of the child as another person. In America, when traveling with a young child, one has to protect the child against being fondled or kissed by strangers less often than in Germany.

The same difference in the basic relationship between the child and the educating adult is found in the schools and nursery schools. Coming from Germany, one notices how slowly and reluctantly a nursery schoolteacher approaches the scene of a tussle between two youngsters. At first such procedure seems almost to indicate a lack of interest on the part of the teacher. But, in fact, the nursery schoolteacher has been taught to follow this procedure. Whenever the teacher wants to interfere with the child's activities, she has to approach the child slowly and gradually. If there is any possibility of settling the problem without her she has to avoid interference. In the progressive German nursery school of the pre-Hitler period the idea of the child's independence was stressed too, especially in the Montessori nursery schools. But the degree of difference in the actual procedure can hardly be exaggerated and is easily noticeable even in the most representative German training schools for nursery schoolteachers. A similarly marked difference exists in regard to a second rule for the American nursery schoolteacher; namely, to be friendly and to speak in a soft voice to the child regardless of his reaction. In Germany, interference of an adult is not only more frequent, but generally more loud and sudden. It occurs much more often in a spirit of command, demanding obedience. I have learned that under the Nazi régime the leading training school for nursery schoolteachers in Germany has to advise its students not to explain an order, even if the child could understand the reason. In this way, the children should get the habit of obeying blindly and absolutely, not from reason, but from belief or love. Such principle is in line with a basic rule of the totalitarian state, which was announced again and again, especially in the first year of its régime: to command those below, to obey those above. Certainly such advice to the nursery schoolteacher goes much farther than that given in pre-Hitler Germany. Nevertheless, one might consider such procedure as an extreme expression of a relation between adult and child which, in comparison with the United States, has always been noticeable in Germany.

The battle of the totalitarian state against reason and intellectual discussion, as "liberalism," is quite logical, because reasoning puts the person involved on a basis of equality. To give reasons in education is therefore a "democratic procedure."

Closely related to the respect for the rights of the child is the tendency of American education to help the child in every way to become practically independent as soon as possible. Much care is taken to develop means and techniques which permit the child to dress himself, to feed and serve himself, and to perform other parts of the daily routine independently. Similar tendencies are common to progressive education in all countries, but the actual freedom of choice and the actual degree of independence intended by the adult, and reached by the child, seem to be considerably higher in the United States than in a comparable German milieu.

All these facts seem to indicate that the space of free movement for the child in American education is greater than in pre-Hitler Germany. Yet there are facts which might make such a conclusion doubtful. American education may recognize the right of the child to a higher degree, yet the American educator certainly cannot be called more compliant than the German one. I was sometimes impressed by the rigidity with which the same nursery schools, which carefully follow the rules mentioned above, will enforce certain procedures. In spite of his greater independence, the American undergraduate, and even the graduate at the university in many respects, stands under more school-like regulations than the German student. The difference between the educational situation in the two countries seems, therefore, to be not only a difference in the amount of free space of movement, but a structural difference as well.

DEGREES OF FREEDOM AND SHARPNESS OF BOUNDARIES

One has to distinguish within a life-space not only regions in which the person is entirely free to act and others which are entirely prohibited, but regions of an intermediate type: A certain activity may not be altogether prohibited, yet the person may feel somewhat restricted and hindered within this region. The different social groups a child belongs to, the atmosphere in the classes of its different teachers, the different social activities in which he is involved are often regions of different *degrees of freedom.*

One finds gradual and abrupt transitions between neighboring regions. The life-space as a whole shows different degrees of homogeneity. There are educational milieus in which, let us say, a medium degree of freedom is characteristic for nearly all regions. A child in a certain boarding school, for example, may not be very much suppressed, yet he may always feel somewhat under regulation. In other cases, the life-space may contain regions of a very high, and others of a very low, degree of freedom. The school, for instance, may be a region of rigid discipline and little freedom, whereas the atmosphere of his family life may be soft and provide plenty of freedom. A similar contrast may exist within the family life of a child as a result of a despotic father and a weak mother. The *degree of homogeneity* of a child's life-space is obviously dynamically important, both for his behavior and his development.

It is furthermore important whether *gradual* or abrupt transitions between neighboring regions prevail in a life-space. The space of free movement of two children may be similar in extent and structure; yet for the one child, the boundaries between the permitted and the forbidden regions may be clearly determined, nearly inflexible, and their recognition strictly enforced. For the second child these boundaries may vary relatively much from day to day (although their position may be on the average the same as for the first child) and may not be very clearly defined. His daily time-schedule may not be punctual. When he is supposed to go to bed he may get permission easily to play just one record and again another record, and then to say goodnight lingeringly, interpolating several jokes before he finally goes to sleep. The frequency and the kind of exceptions granted to a child vary greatly. The reaction of the parents to a child's demand may be a clear-cut yes or no, whereas another child may get all degrees of intermediate answers. In other words, the prevailing sharpness of the boundaries between neighboring regions vary greatly.

The educational situation in the United States as compared to Germany seems to be characterized by *regions of very different degrees of freedom and sharply determined boundaries of these regions* (Figures Ia and Ib). In a Froebel nursery school in Germany, for example, the child is usually more guided and regulated in his play and his outdoor activities than in a comparable American nursery school. The American nursery school, on the other hand, is more likely to emphasize the necessity of strict rules for the daily routines, e.g., at meals. On the whole, it seems that the educational atmosphere in German institutions, as well as in German homes, is more *homogeneous*, lacking regions of such a high degree of freedom, and having less strictly defined limits than are found in a similar institution or home in the United

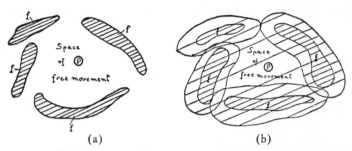

(a)   (b)

FIGURE I.   TYPICAL SITUATIONS OF AN EDUCATIONAL ATMOSPHERE
(a) THE UNITED STATES (b) GERMANY

(a) Life-space with sharp boundaries and great qualitative differences between neighboring regions.
(b) Life-space with unsharp boundaries and relatively small differences between neighboring regions.
The density of the hatching represents the degree of restriction.
P=person f=forbidden region

States. The new totalitarian Germany, of course, has taken decisive steps to increase the homogeneity in education, as well as in every other field, thus creating an all-inclusive, highly regulated situation.

Besides its greater heterogeneity the life-space of the American educational situation seems to have *sharper boundaries* between its different regions. I have mentioned already that American education considers it a main issue to create in the young child a habit of greatest punctuality in the daily routine. That implies a sharp boundary of an important group of daily activities in the life-space of the child. A similar time structure is characteristic for the American student. The student at the American university is likely to have a fixed time-schedule worked out in advance for a much longer period and in greater detail than does the German student. He may plan the number of hours he will spend per week on research for a period of six months ahead. He sets strict time limitations on his work more often than a student in a similar social and scientific position in Germany. It is more likely that a student will forget time limitations and lose himself in his work in Germany than in the United States (this fact is not due to a higher economic pressure on the American student). The common use of examinations at least every half year, unknown in the German university, does a good deal for cutting the work at the American university into well-defined regions.

THE STRUCTURE OF AMERICAN EDUCATION AS AN EXPRESSION OF THE AMERICAN STYLE OF LIVING

I have mentioned in the beginning that the educational situation and the educational procedure are to a high degree determined by the social situation of the country as a whole. The prospective teacher, of course, learns pedagogical reasons for the techniques he is supposed to apply; they are claimed to be favorable for the development of the child. In fact, the good American nursery school is in my judgment pedagogically better than that of any other country. Yet one will have to realize that the procedure in the American nursery school is, at least to a high degree, not the result of scientific psychology, but an expression of the American style of living and of the more empirical way the American tests his technique of handling human beings. To some degree, one can find the main characteristics of the educational situation probably in every field of American life.

The most common epithet given to the United States in Europe is: "the country of great contrasts," "country of unlimited possibilities." The moving frontier has offered freedom, the possibility to leave disliked places. Even today the American citizen is much more ready to shift his home to a new district than the German of a similar social group. This willingness to shift distinguishes, for example, the American farmer very distinctly from the peasant in the comparatively narrow and overcrowded Germany.

There are large regions of activities in which the average American is very free. Yet, if he steps over certain boundaries which are relatively sharply defined, he will find himself quite forcefully treated. The same abrupt transition which we find in American education is observable in other fields of social life. For example, one notices the way the policeman conducts himself with extreme politeness or extreme roughness ("third degree") according to the situation. Like the American climate, the American economic and social life includes extremes (the biggest and best even in crime). The American does not mind, or even prefers, extremes in close proximity. In business life, the American seems more inclined to take risks, selling or buying on a large scale. One is more accustomed to someone's getting rich or poor quickly.

The various regions of activity within the social life of the United States seem to be more circumscribed, more clearly distinguished and more sharply separated than in Germany. In America, two scientists or politicians may emerge from a hard theoretical or political fight and yet be on cordial terms with each other. In Germany, for most persons, a political or even a scientific disagreement seems to be inseparable from moral disapproval. The congratulations that the defeated candidate for the presidency sends to the elected, after a hard battle, would sound rather strange in Germany. It is another side of the same separation of regions of activity that certain social groups regard each other as equals in politics and business, but have nearly no connection in social life.

In his relation to time, the American shows a definite tendency to cut the field into sharply defined and separated regions: the people of the United States are more punctual than Europeans and take punctuality much more seriously. That a dozen guests who have been invited to an informal dinner party at seven all arrive between 7:00 and 7:08 is as unheard of in Germany as it is common in the United States. The luncheon gatherings with lectures or entertainments, which are so popular in the United States and practically unknown in Germany, would not be possible if the American public had not been accustomed to well-defined time-steps. The common American saying: "This work will take me so and so many minutes" is seldom heard in Germany, where people involved in work or play forget more often about the time altogether. Some American popular journals print the reading time of every article at the beginning.

On the whole, the differentiation of the educational situation into relatively contrasting regions with sharp boundaries seems to be characteristic for large fields of social life. Also the greater respect for the child seems to have its parallels in the general American social life. The average American seems to be much more hesitant to interfere with any situation in which somebody else is involved. If a German store is full of customers, the clerk will try to hasten from one to another, and he will be frequently approached with questions from one customer while he is busy with another. The American clerk, even under such conditions, usually grants to each customer enough time for a leisurely decision while the other customers are waiting patiently. The same "fairness" toward other persons can be seen at the bank or at the post office during rush hours. A similar attitude determines the behavior of the average car driver toward a pedestrian who is crossing the street or toward a slowly driven car which he is unable to pass. On all such occasions the German is much more likely to become impatient, aggressive, and emotional. Not to stop a car when a pedestrian wants to cross a street would be considered reckless or at least impolite in the United States under conditions in which it would be customary in Germany. The person in the car feels, in Germany, "naturally" superior to the pedestrian, and expects the pedestrian to wait. The pedestrian on the other side joins "naturally" in this feeling and waits, in contrast to the American pedestrian.

Such cases are small yet significant criteria for the greater "respect" which the American has for the other individual. They show that the aversion against interfering with children, which we have mentioned in the educational fields, is but an expression of a different basic relation between the individuals in the United States and Germany. This difference is obviously closely related to the American's ideal of democracy, to the idea that fundamentally every person has the same right, regardless of whether he is rich or poor, the President, or an average citizen. The same lack of submissiveness which appears in the relation between child and adult is characteristic of the behavior of the American employee toward his employer, or of the student toward his professor. As an illustration, I may use a German working in a minor position in one of the German consulates in the United States. After the war he returned to Germany, working in a similar position in the governmental administration. His colleagues frequently told him that he did not "behave properly" toward his superiors. In spite of his best intentions such mistakes of "impoliteness" occurred again and again. So he soon went back to his position in the United States, saying, "There we obey every order as well as in Germany, yet outside our obligation, we feel less inferior." (This happened in the pre-Hitler period.)

That the German children in the streetcar are supposed to offer their seats to the adults, a behavior no longer requested of American children of this generation, is only one of the many expressions of this different basic relation between individuals. Germans, even in the short period between monarchy and Fascism, were influenced more constantly by the relation of superior and inferior than are Americans. The democratic idea of equal rights in the United States goes so far that one sometimes seems to ascribe even the same abilities to every person and to consider lack of success a proof of moral inferiority. In the same direction points the ideal of self-sufficiency of every individual. It makes the adolescent more eager than in Germany to become self-sustaining as soon as possible. It seems to be one of the reasons why American well-to-do fathers are willing to give huge sums to public institutions. A generosity of such degree is unknown in Germany, where fathers are more eager to preserve as much as possible for their children.

APPARENT CONTRADICTIONS

The properties of the educational and general social life which I have mentioned seem to be in line with each other, at least in

so far as they do not contradict each other. But it would be mis-
leading not to mention some trends, both in education and in
other social fields, which seem to point somewhat in opposite
directions. In spite of the democratic idea of equality of men,
proclaimed in the American constitution as one of its basic principles, there are probably no other people as interested in *individual accomplishments*, in sports, movies and elsewhere, and as
ready to honor such individuals in every way as the Americans.
The interest in individual differences is in American education
distinctly greater than in Germany. Tests concerning individual
differences are much further developed and are applied on a
much larger scale than in any other country. This fact is mainly the
result of the genuine interest which the educational system and
the general public takes in "personality." Every newspaper is full
of society news, pictures of debutantes and brides, pictures of
leaders, or distinguished students at the universities and high
schools. Newspapers in smaller towns publish good achievements
of a school child such as perfect spelling and arithmetic papers.
All this is practically unknown in Germany. The interest in personal achievement has decidedly determined the development of
American psychology, and is one of the reasons why the "social
status" of psychology is much higher in the United States than
in Germany (even in the pre-Hitler period), where philosophy
is considered as much more important than psychology.

A second point, which might seem not in line with the facts
mentioned above, is the homogeneity of American social life. We
have spoken about the differentiation of the educational and the
general social situation in contrasting regions with sharp boundaries. Yet in some respects the social life in the United States
seems to be much more homogeneous than in Germany. The
architecture and the character of the towns and villages varies decidedly more in Germany than in the United States. Despite Germany's smaller size and the new immigrant groups in the United
States, the differences in language and in habits between the
people in various parts of the country seem to be greater in Germany. I have mentioned already that the differences between social

classes and other historically determined social groups commonly is considered to be greater in Germany. The same chain stores can be found in every village throughout the United States. American hotels differ much less than German ones. Standardization is further developed. The whole social life in the United States shows some kind of uniformity.

THEORETICAL INTERPRETATION
HISTORICAL AND SYSTEMATIC EXPLANATION

One can try to explain the different properties of American and German social life historically. It is a valuable and important task to follow every step of the historical development which has led to a society with just such characteristics. But to answer, for instance, such problems as the influence of a special culture on the growing child, one has to answer besides, and one may say first, another problem. One has to face the educational situation with all its social and cultural implications as *one concrete dynamic whole.* One will have to understand the dynamic interrelations between the various parts and properties of the situation in which, and as part of which, the child is living. In other words, there should be a systematic explanation, besides the "historical" one, namely, an explanation of how these different parts and properties can exist within one concrete social whole. As in psychology, in sociology both the historical and the systematic question "why" is important, and neither question is finally to be solved without the other. Yet they are considerably different from the logical point of view, and the systematic explanation often has to be considered first.

If one wishes to understand the interrelation between the parts and properties of a situation, the possibility of their coexistence, and its possible effects upon its various parts (e.g., upon a child's development), it is necessary to analyze the situation. But this analysis must be a "gestalt-theoretical" one, because the social situation, like the psychological situation, is a dynamic whole. It means that a change of one of its parts implies a change of the other parts.

It seems possible to interrelate several of the properties of American and German social life by using as a starting-point and center of the derivation, a certain assumption about the difference between the American and the German person as a social being. In this case, differences concerning groups would logically be derived from certain differences among their members.

I am eager to prevent any misunderstanding which may be attached to such a procedure. Using a statement about individuals as the *logical* center for the derivation does not imply that the differences between individuals are the *cause* of the differences of the group and its social life. On the contrary, I am convinced that the difference in the structure of the individual in Germany and in the United States is itself a result of his living in a different social set-up built by different histories. I think there is ample proof for this statement.

THE SOCIAL DISTANCE BETWEEN INDIVIDUALS IN THE UNITED STATES AND IN GERMANY

Considering the structure of the individual as a social being, there seem to be the following differences between the typical American and typical German. The average *"social distance"* (the term used as in sociology) *between different individuals seems to be smaller in the United States so far as the surface regions,* or, as one may say, the *"peripheral regions" of the personality are concerned.* That means the American is more willing to be open to other individuals and to share certain situations with other individuals than the German.

Quite commonly strangers on the street may greet one another with a smile, a behavior unusual in Germany. People waiting for the bus may start to discuss the weather, and in the train, conversation between strangers starts more easily than in Germany. (There is certainly a difference between the people of a large and a small town, both in the United States and Germany. The Englishman, at least outside of England, may be even more reserved in such situations than a German.) The American seems more friendly and more ready to help a stranger. It is more customary in the United States to invite a visitor, who is not a personal friend, to lunch or to one's home, than in Germany under similar circumstances. Nearly every German coming to the United States admires the natural ease and the efficiency with which the Americans generally take care of all the minor difficulties a newcomer has to face.

In boarding houses, one finds people sitting in their rooms with the door wide open, so that anyone might step in. The American seems to have decidedly less need for privacy in certain regions of life. It is possible to find the office door of even a president of a college open all day; so everybody can see with whom he is conversing and in what manner he is acting. Such behavior would be unthinkable in Germany even for an unimportant official, one of whose techniques in getting respect and showing his importance is to let people wait a long time in front of his closed door. In the United States it would be bad taste to let other persons wait, however great the difference in the social status of the persons involved may be. This difference between the United States and Germany is very striking, and is an expression of the democratic attitude toward the equal rights of everybody and of the greater general accessibility of the American.

The average American talks less loudly than the German, both in a private conversation, and in public. It may well be that this is due to the fact that the peripheral regions of the U-type are more accessible. Besides, the G-type tends, as we will see, to a more emotional and aggressive behavior. (See Figure III, page 22.)

Nevertheless, the average "social distance" between persons in the United States seems not to be smaller in every respect, but only in regard to more peripheral layers of the person. The more intimate "central" regions of personality seem to be at least as separated between different persons, and at least as difficult to get access to as among Germans. For instance, relations between boys and girls might progress in the United States more easily up to a certain point, whereas the step leading to an intimate relationship seems to be more clearly marked than in Germany. In

Germany, there is a more gradual transition in social relationships from the very peripheral to the very intimate. Germans entering the United States notice usually that the degree of friendly and close relation, which one may achieve as a newcomer within a few weeks, is much higher than under similar circumstances in Germany. Compared with Germans, Americans seem to make quicker progress towards friendly relations in the beginning, and with many more persons. Yet this development often stops at a certain point; and the quickly acquired friends will, after years of relatively close relations, say good-by as easily as after a few weeks of acquaintance.

AN OPERATIONAL DEFINITION OF SOCIAL DISTANCE

If one wants to express these facts with topological and dynamic concepts, one has to ask what "social distance" between persons means from an operational point of view.

Two groups of facts seem to be possible for an operational definition of social distances:

1. One can start with the difference between the more "peripheral" and the more "central" regions of the person, taking the operational definition from the many kinds of experiments in which the relation of an activity to these different layers have proved to be of primary importance (experiments on psychological satiation, emotions, quasi-needs). The more central regions are defined as the more intimate, personal regions. In these regions, the individual usually is more sensitive than in the peripheral.

2. The second definition could make use of the way social distances generally are proved in sociology: The person A is asked whether he would share certain situations (like traveling in the same car, playing games together, dancing together, marrying) with a certain person B. The differences in social distance can be defined as different degrees of intimacy of the situation which the person is willing to share with the other.

A certain distance, therefore, means, dynamically speaking, the accessibility of certain situations or activities of the person B for the person A, and the non-accessibility for more intimate situations. This accessibility to certain situations or activities is equivalent (or very closely related) to the possibility of B to communicate with certain, but not with the more central, layers of A.

So far as the state of the person A is concerned, a smaller social distance to B than to C means that more central regions of A are open to B than to C. The statement about the typical American compared with the typical German would mean that, *ceteris paribus*, the peripheral layers of the American show less resistance against communication from another person.

One can represent the greater "openness" by co-ordinating to the peripheral layers themselves or to their boundaries less resist-

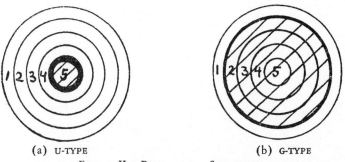

(a) U-TYPE	(b) G-TYPE

FIGURE II. PERSONALITY STRUCTURE

The thickness of the boundary lines between the personality layers represents the difference in accessibility. The hatched area corresponds to the "private" region of the person.

ance against communicative actions from outside. Figure II represents the state of the typical American (U-type, Figure IIa) com· pared with the German (G-type, Figure IIb).

In the diagram, the degree of resistance against communica· tion from outside is represented by stronger boundaries (heavier lines) around the layer in question. I distinguish arbitrarily the same number of layers within the person.

Using such means, one would have to symbolize the U-type, let us say, by four peripheral regions with easily permeable boundaries. Only the very central (fifth) region is insulated from

communication to a high degree. In the G-type only the most peripheral region (first) is easily accessible. The more central are
relatively difficult of approach. A major boundary lies already
between the regions 1 and 2 (Figure IIb).

The facts available seem not to permit a statement about the
relative permeability of every region. But they do seem to permit
statements about position of the first main resistance against *invasion* from outside.

If the same effort which is necessary in a certain situation to
communicate with the region 1 of a G-type would suffice to reach

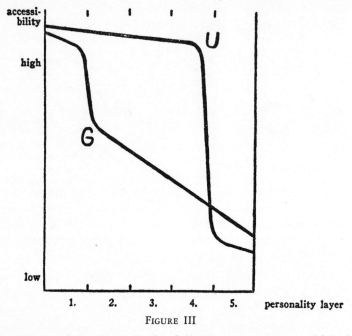

FIGURE III

the region 4 of the U-type, the following equation would hold:
$W(1+2+3)_U = W(1)_G$ (W means the resistance of a zone; U,
the person of United States; and G, the person of Germany). It
can furthermore be stated that $W(1+2)_U < W(1+2)_G$. This
means that the resistance offered by the given number of peripheral
layers is less in the U-type than in the G-type.

Several facts seem to indicate that the *most intimate* region (fifth) is generally less accessible in the U-type than in the G-type. In this case $W(1+2+3+4)_U > W(1+2+3+4)_G$ would hold. We will not assume this fact in our further derivation. In any case, even if the degree of accessibility of the most intimate region (fifth) would be about the same $[W(1+2+3+4)_U = W(1+2+3+4)_G]$, the dynamic boundary between region 4_U and 5_U would probably have to be stronger than between 1_G and 2_G.

On the whole, the decrease in accessibility from the peripheral to the central regions seems to correspond in Germany more to curve G (Figure III), in the United States more to curve U.

PRIVATE AND NON-PRIVATE PERSONAL REGIONS

If one considers the accessibility of the different regions not from the point of view of two individuals, but from that of the group, one will have to ascribe to the more peripheral regions the field of open, common, "public" life of the individual, to the more central regions the field of private life of the individual. This granted, one can conclude from our basic thesis that more regions of the persons are considered of public interest in the United States than in Germany.

It seems to me that this statement can be illustrated by facts. Newspapers in the United States are full of descriptions of the clothes persons wore at certain occasions, who was invited for dinner by whom, and of the table decorations. As we mentioned above, in many respects more publicity is given to facts which would be considered private and of no public interest in comparable newspapers in Germany. Even informal gatherings have often a less intimate, private character than similar occasions in Germany. The techniques of make-up are discussed in the newspapers noticeably more often and in a more detailed manner in the United States.

EMOTION, FRIENDSHIP, AND FRICTION

A second fact could be mentioned which is somewhat related to the same structural differences. The American is much less likely to respond with anger, or at least with open anger, to the hundred small misfortunes of everyday life. Several facts seem to converge to this effect. The American reacts generally to such accidents more from the point of view of action (he considers what has to be done next in order to remedy the situation), the German more from a moral point of view (he considers whose fault it was). Furthermore, such incidents are less likely to touch central regions of the person. In other words, the range of events which correspond to the peripheral, non-private regions, seems to be comparatively greater for the American. This is entirely in line with our basic statement. As the private field includes more layers for the G-type, he is likely to act more emotionally.

This fact is of especial importance for the interrelationship be-

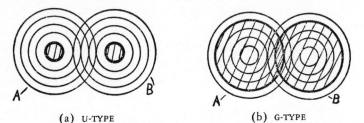

(a) U-TYPE   (b) G-TYPE

FIGURE IV. TWO PERSONS (A AND B) IN COMMUNICATION

tween several persons. One can ask how many layers of two persons (A and B, Figure IV) can come in contact with each other without touching the "private" regions. Communication between regions can be represented by overlapping, or by a common boundary of the regions in question. From our basic assumption, it follows that more regions can overlap in the U-type than in the G-type before private regions are touched. For instance, the overlapping of the three outer layers does not involve a communication between the private regions of the U-type (Figure IVa), whereas such overlapping would involve private regions of the G-type (Figure IVb).

This should have two results: It should make possible *relatively close relations between persons of the U-type without a deep personal friendship.* On the other hand, these persons should be *less in danger of personal friction.* Such friction occurs more easily if personal regions are touched. The facts mentioned seem to be well in line with both conclusions.

ACTIONS AND IDEALS

The fact that there are more regions which are not considered "private" by the American does not mean that these peripheral regions are considered of less importance by him. On the contrary, if one considers the structure of the person as a whole, our basic assumption implies that the relative weight of the non-private regions is greater for a person of the U-type than for the G-type. The facts mentioned above point already in this direction.

A second fact can be mentioned here. The peripheral layers of personality include what one can call the "motoric" or "executive" region of a person. This region is the outer layer of the person, the one closest to the environment. It corresponds to the appearance and action of the person. That the relative weight of the appearance seems to be greater for the U-type was mentioned above. The *actions* are relatively more emphasized in the U-type. The American, as compared with the German, emphasizes achievement more than ideology or status. In science he emphasizes practice more than theory. The U-type prefers to make extensive "empirical" collections of facts. The greater relative weight which the central regions, and therefore the ideals and other "irreal" facts have for the German, is of fundamental importance for so-called German idealism as against American pragmatism. A similar difference in attitude between Germans and Americans is striking in the fields of politics and religion.

THE DEGREE OF HOMOGENEITY WITHIN A GROUP

If the central regions correspond to the more private life and the more peripheral regions to his open, "public" life, the latter should be more similar among individuals of the same social group than the former. For, without sufficient similarity of the regions, mutually accessible to most of the members of the group, the common intercourse and common social life would not be possible. (This holds true only to a certain degree.)

It may be that the most intimate regions contain so much of general human nature that they again are relatively alike among persons. In this case, the greatest dissimilarity among individuals within one group would exist between their regions of medium privacy.

The sum of the regions which show this degree of similarity would be greater for the group as a whole within a sample of 1,000 Americans than of 1,000 Germans. This can be derived in the following way: The average degree of similarity (DS) of the region $(1+2+3)$ among the members of the U-group (Figure

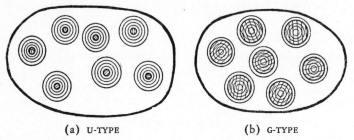

(a) U-TYPE   (b) G-TYPE

FIGURE V.   HOMOGENEITY OF THE GROUP

Va) may be designated $DS\frac{3}{U}$. The average degree of similarity DS_G^3 of the corresponding region $(1+2+3)$ would be smaller among the G-group $(DS\frac{3}{U} > DS_G^3)$, for this region would already lie partly within the private zones of the G-type (Figure Vb) but not of the U-type. In other words, to a given degree of similarity (DS) correspond more inclusive regions in the U-type than in the G-type. The sum(Σ) of regions (r) up to this degree of similarity (r^{DS}) in the group as a whole is greater in the U-sample than in the G-sample: $\Sigma r_U^{DS} > \Sigma r_G^{DS}$. *This means the U-group is more homogeneous than the G-group* in respect to a greater number of personality regions.

It may be noted that a statement regarding the homogeneity of the members of a group does not include a definite statement about the organization of the group as a whole.

One can make the same conclusion from our basic statement about the different personality structures, without taking the trouble of detailed derivation by referring to the geometrical representations (Figures Va and Vb): For a given number of different individuals a,b,c,d, . . . the amount of private regions within the group as a whole is greater in the G-group than in the U-group. This conclusion is in line with the direct observations about the greater homogeneity which we have mentioned above.

THE DEGREE OF SIMILARITY OF MEMBERS OF DIFFERENT GROUPS

Given two groups in the same country, each homogeneous in itself, but different from each other, what is *ceteris paribus* the degree of similarity between members of such groups in the United States and in Germany?

One can answer this question best by considering an extreme case of full homogeneity within each group. In this case, the members (a^1, a^2, a^3, . . .) of the one group (A) would be all alike: $a^1 = a^2 = a^3 = \ldots$. The same would hold for the members b^1, b^2, b^3, . . . of the second group (B): ($b^1 = b^2 = b^3 \ldots$). Figures VIa and VIb represent two such ideal groups both in the United States and in Germany. They show, at the same time, that the difference between the members of the two groups would be greater in Germany, for the amount of personality regions alike in both groups is greater in the United States. In other words, the probable difference of two homogeneous groups is greater in Germany than in the United States.

Observation seems to justify this conclusion relatively often. It has been stated frequently that distinct "classes" with generally recognized and fixed social status are more pronounced in Germany than in the United States.

GROUP SIZE

Closely related to this deduction is a second derivation of group properties from the personality structure of its members.

It is probably not possible to make a general statement concerning the optimum degree of similarity between members of a social group. This degree is different, e.g., for a club which is fundamentally based upon and sustained by the will of the mem-

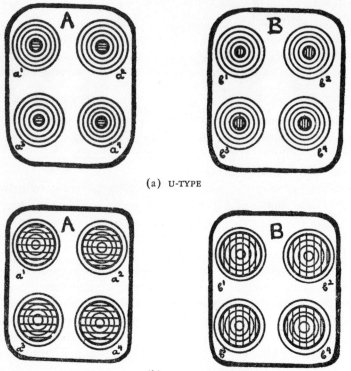

(a) U-TYPE

(b) G-TYPE

FIGURE VI.   DEGREE OF SIMILARITY BETWEEN MEMBERS OF TWO
DIFFERENT GROUPS A AND B

bers to associate, and on the other hand for a military group, which is sustained by the command of an officer. Nevertheless, there are groups of the first type, which presuppose a sufficient similarity between their members. If the individual differences within such a group become too great, the group will split; if the difference of the prospective newcomer from the average member is too great, the person will have to remain outside the group.

From our basic assumption it follows that the number of persons which can enter such a group is comparatively greater in the United States than in Germany. To enter a club or a political party means that one is willing to share certain actions with its other members. In accordance with the statements on page 26 above one should find among a thousand persons of the U-type taken at random a greater number willing to co-operate in a certain (not too intimate) field of activity than among a thousand persons of the G-type. Referring to the graphical representation (Figure VI), one can say: The adding of a single new person increases (on the average) the total amount of individual differences within a group more in a G-group than in a U-group. If, therefore, the amount of dissimilarity bearable for a group is limited this point is reached earlier within a G-group.

This conclusion also seems to fit the facts very well. Practically only two large political parties exist in the United States, whereas the political life in Germany has shown more than a dozen political parties. These individualistic trends have often been emphasized. ("Wherever three Germans come together, they found four associations.")

A second reason for splitting into relatively small and differentiated groups is the greater emphasis of ideas relative to action (page 25). The small number of Socialist votes in the American presidential election in 1932, e.g., was partly due to a tendency among Socialists, "not to waste their vote" for a candidate who would not win. One hears the expression of such a "practical" attitude much more frequently in the United States than in Germany. The G-type under similar circumstances was more likely to vote according to his ideals than in reference to a certain action.

We have mentioned that similarly individualistic trends of the G-type can be observed in relation to social gatherings. This fact can also be understood as the result of a greater amount of individual differences within the region $(1+2+3+4)$ of the G-type. The greater amount of individual differences among the regions

$(2+3+4)$ and their minor accessibility decrease the number of people among which the G-type feels comfortable in a party.

PERSONS IN DIFFERENT SITUATIONS

One can ask how much the U-type and the G-type will be affected by changes of the situation. This problem is related to questions mentioned in the beginning, but it is not easy to make clear derivations from our basic assumptions.

The person A may change from Situation I to the different Situation II (Figure VII). The degree to which a person will be affected by this change depends not only upon the degree of difference between the Situations I and II, but also upon the kind of situations, and further, upon what one means by "change of a person."

Within the limitations following from these facts one can say: As the U-type has more layers which are relatively accessible, on

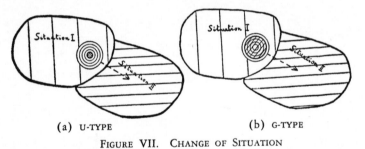

(a) U-TYPE   (b) G-TYPE

FIGURE VII.   CHANGE OF SITUATION

the average, more layers of this type than of the G-type will be influenced by a change of the situation (Figure VIIa). That means the U-type (Figure VIIa) shows a greater difference in his behavior in accordance with the given situation than the G-type (Figure VIIb). Indeed, the German *Geheimrat* behaves as *Geheimrat* in every situation. (Grosz's caricature of two officials meeting in bathing suits, but nevertheless showing all the formalities of behavior, will be less appropriate for the United States.) We have previously mentioned (page 23) several facts which all point in the same direction: The greater area of private regions within the

G-type means that he carries more of his specific individual characteristics to every situation. His behavior will therefore be less modified in altered situations. We have mentioned the fact that the behavior of the U-type separates more clearly the different fields of life. His greater "fluidity" and his tendency to go from one extreme to the opposite could be understood to a large degree from this greater dependability upon the situation because these changes in behavior occur generally as a response to a change of the situation.

A special application of the same rule could be related to the so-called rugged individualism of the American people. We have mentioned the apparent discrepancy between the greater accessibility of the U-type and his greater ease in making contacts on the one hand, his carefulness to avoid any kind of interference on the other hand. Closer consideration seems to show that this difference can be understood as another example of a strong reaction to a situation: If A is outside a situation which has for him the character of belonging to the private sphere of B, he will be more reluctant to enter than the G-type, because he respects more the difference of these situations.

We mentioned in the beginning that more of the peripheral layers are easily accessible in the U-type, but that the private, central layers may be even less accessible. The respect for situations belonging to the private sphere of another person, and the rigidity and jealousy with which the own private sphere is guarded shows that a similarly great difference holds for the situations, objects, and events belonging to these spheres. We will come back to this problem, when we discuss the distribution of power in both countries.

We have seen that social life in the United States seems to be, on the one hand, more homogeneous, but, on the other hand, its different regions seem to be more separated. These facts which may at first seem to be somewhat contradictory can now be understood as in accordance with each other: the social group shows a greater homogeneity in the United States. That means there are less differences between its sub-groups or its members. But the behavior of the same sub-group or the same individual will be less constant in different situations than in Germany and social life will therefore be more "fluid" in the United States.

Yet this statement needs some qualification. It is more likely that more peripheral layers of the U-type are touched by a situation. But from our basic assumption follows also that there is less likelihood that the "private" layers of the U-type than of the G-type become involved. In fact, the U-type is, as we have seen, less likely to react emotionally; he is more often able to keep his relation to the situation within the more peripheral layers of "action." He can more easily than the G-type preserve himself against being personally deeply entangled; he can keep his intimate central region more easily outside and therefore "above" the situation. It may well be that the greater punctuality and the better technical organization of his activities are partly due to this fact.

It may be well to emphasize that *sharpness* and dynamic *rigidity* of boundaries should not be confused. A field may be divided into regions of great contrast, and these contrasting regions may be directly adjacent (as represented in Figure IIa). In this case, one has to deal with sharp boundaries. Nevertheless, considering the ease with which the field can be changed, the field may have to be called fluid: it may require only small forces to change the boundaries and the whole structure of the field. Sharp boundaries may or may not offer great resistance against locomotions; in other words, they may or may not be rigid.

On the other hand, fields with less contrasting regions and unsharp boundaries (Figure Ib) can be, at the same time, less fluid. Unsharp boundaries may, nevertheless, be difficult to pass, and rigid. Of course, they can be fluid too.

The American is proud of his ability to "take it." The German, too, has learned that a real man and fighter has to be able to stand severe blows. Yet the way this is accomplished seems to be typically different: The G-type is able to take it by appealing to his highest duty, and by throwing his whole person into the task. The U-type, on the contrary, tries to take it by keeping his personal layers as much as possible out, in other words, by "taking it easy," by "taking it with a smile" as a good sport. This difference is related to a different attitude concerning rights and duties in both societies.

To prevent misunderstandings we may be permitted to state again certain goals which have guided us in writing this. The different characteristics ascribed to the United States and to Germany should be taken as tentative descriptions. The differences mentioned are all differences in degree; they show a great variability within each country and may hold true only within certain groups. We did not include the Negro problem and other minority problems.

The description deals only with the present situation without statement as to its duration or its history. The attempt to reveal some logical interrelations between certain characteristics of social groups and of their members as social beings does not answer historical questions of causation, but deals with "systematic" questions of dynamic interrelations exclusively.

2

CULTURAL RECONSTRUCTION

(1943)

BUILDING a world of peace which will be worth at least the name "better than before" includes many problems: political, economic, and cultural. Each of them is loaded with difficulties. Yet all of them have to be considered together and attacked together as interdependent aspects of one dynamic field if any successful step forward is to be achieved.

The implications of the cultural aspect seem to be particularly unclear. Has the culture of the German, the Japanese, the British, or Chinese anything to do with their likelihood or unlikelihood of going to war as an aggressor or fighting in a certain way when hard pressed? Are these cultural differences of any importance for intercultural co-operation?

The discussion of this question seems to have been retarded by philosophical and political sentiments. The difference between peoples has either been overemphasized and treated as innate racial characteristics, or underemphasized and treated as unessential, frequently by misinterpreting the democratic doctrine of equal rights of men. A realistic, scientific approach will have to consider differences between modern cultures as facts of the same nature as differences between "primitive" cultures. Such a scientific approach will refuse to consider cultural characteristics unalterable in principle. Instead, it will ask in an empirical fashion: How easily and with what methods can a certain degree of cultural change be accomplished and how permanent does such a change promise to be?

Definite answers to such questions can be supplied only by an "experimental cultural anthropology" which will study cultural changes systematically under specially created conditions. Unfortunately, cultural anthropology is still in its "descriptive" stage; it has its hands full with finding methods of observing and describing modern cultures adequately and reliably. There have been but inklings of experiments about how cultures can actively be changed in a desired direction. Nevertheless, we will have to try to do the best we can.

A certain amount of cultural reconstruction will be necessary in most countries after the war; these countries will have to switch from a wartime to a peacetime "culture." Most nations will have to be able to do this without help from the outside. This shift from wartime to peacetime culture should be less difficult than it might appear in view of the present hatred, particularly if peace should bring about a decent political world organization. After the last war sizable proportions of the population in most countries turned quickly to a radical pacifism. This experience should warn us not to confuse the violence of a cultural sentiment with its depths and permanency. In this country, the let-down after the last war quickly turned into isolationism, thus setting the stage for this war. (The danger of a similar reaction after this war is again probably greater than that of a permanent imperialistic militarism in this country.) Even in Germany right after the last war the proportion of the population which turned to pacifism was probably larger than the group which started immediately to build for revenge and as a first step invented the *Dolchstosslegende*. (The home front was said to have stabbed the army in the back; in this way the prestige of the German army was maintained.)

The fact that superficial although violent cultural sentiments might change quickly in a nation does not, however, disprove those historians who claim that nothing can be changed so little as the deeper cultural characteristics of a people. It is these deeper cultural traits which we have to consider when thinking of the

cultural aspects of permanent peace. In Germany, in spite of the
pacifistic sentiment after the First World War and long before
Hitler, every child was again playing war with toy soldiers. And
soon, in line with long-standing tradition, militarists were again
winning out. On the other hand, Mussolini has tried for more than
a decade to build up in the Italians those soldierly characteristics
which were obviously lacking in the First World War. In spite of
a very thorough attempt which reached every age level down to
early childhood he seems to have failed to alter these cultural
characteristics. Similarly, certain peculiarities of the Russian or the
British character seem to change very little. That these permanent
characteristics are cultural rather than racial is shown by the fact
that children taken from one country to the other will quickly and
thoroughly adopt the characteristics of the people in the new
country.

A democratic world order does not require or even favor cultural
uniformity all over the world. The parallel to democratic freedom
for the individual is cultural pluralism for groups. But any democratic society has to safeguard against misuse of individual freedom
by the gangster or—politically speaking—the "intolerant." Without establishing to some degree the principle of tolerance, of
equality of rights, in every culture the "intolerant" culture will
always be endangering a democratic world organization. Intolerance against intolerant cultures is therefore a prerequisite to any
organization of permanent peace.

To encourage change toward democracy a change of values in a
vast realm would have to be accomplished. This change would
include, for instance, increased emphasis on human values as
against superhuman values, such as the state, politics, science. It
would emphasize what the German "Iron Chancellor" Bismarck
called far back in 1880 *Civilcourage* (morale courage of the civil-
ians) and what he deplored as lacking in the German character
(as against the courage and the blind obedience of the soldier).
It would stress the value of manipulating difficulties rather than
complaining about them. It would stress education for independence rather than for obedience.

In any attempt to influence cultural patterns it cannot be emphasized too much that the problem of changing single persons or small groups which are uprooted and transplanted into a new cultural background is rather different from the problem of changing the culture of a compact group remaining on native soil. The technique which seems to offer itself as the natural means to reach such a compact group for the purpose of changing the cultural backgrounds is "propaganda" in its various forms, such as radio, newspaper, etc.

However, even if such propaganda from outside or inside the country were successful it would not be likely to do much more than change the "verbal sentiments" of a people. When speaking about "democracy" the German is likely to mean individualistic freedom. If an American defines democracy he too very frequently stresses individualistic freedom and forgets that leadership is fully as important in a democracy as in an autocracy. But the American happens to live in a country where the efficiency of the process of group decisions is relatively highly developed, at least in small groups, and where democratic leadership is thoroughly accepted as a cultural pattern and taught in practice to children in school. One cannot expect people living in a country without such traditions to understand a term like democracy in any other way than in those conceptual dimensions in which they are accustomed to think. One cannot expect the member of a different culture to accept a never-experienced cultural pattern which even the people who have experienced that pattern are seldom able to describe adequately. It has been one of the tragedies of the German Republic that the democratically minded people who were in power immediately after the war confused democracy with "being unpolitical" and under this slogan permitted the old reactionaries to keep their official positions as "experts." It was a tragedy that they did not know that "intolerance against the intolerant" is as essential for maintaining and particularly for establishing a democracy as "tolerance for the tolerant"; above all, it was a tragedy that they did not know that strong leadership and an efficient positive use of the political power by the majority is an essential aspect of democracy. Instead, Germany congratulated herself on having "the freest Constitution in the world" because technically even a small minority gets its proportional representation in the parliament. Actually, this set-up led to dozens of political parties and to the permanent domination of the majority by a minority group in the center.

A second main obstacle against changing cultures is the fact that a pattern like democracy is not limited to political problems but is interwoven with every aspect of the culture. How the mother handles her child of one, two, or three years of age; how business is conducted; what group has status; how status differences are reacted to—all of these habitudes are essential elements of the cultural pattern. Every major change, therefore, has to be carried through against such a highly interwoven background. It cannot be limited to a change in officially recognized values; it has to be a change in actual group life.

While it is correct that change of values will finally lead to a change of social conduct, it is equally correct that changes of action patterns and of actual group life will change cultural values. This indirect change of cultural values probably reaches deeper and is more permanent than direct changes of values by propaganda. There is no need to point out how thoroughly Hitler has understood this fact. Is there any hope of influencing Fascist group life in a direction toward democracy?

The scientific research in this field, although meager, seems to warrant at least a few general statements:

1. It is a fallacy to assume that people, if left alone, follow a democratic pattern in their group life. Such an assumption would not even hold for people living in a democratic society. (The development of certain countries, like the United States, toward democracy was a result of very unique historical-geographical conditions.) In democracy, as in any culture, the individual acquires the cultural pattern by some type of "learning." Normally, such learning occurs by way of growing up in that culture.

2. In regard to changing from one cultural pattern to another experiments indicate that autocracy can be "imposed upon a per-

son." That means the individual might "learn" autocracy by adapting himself to a situation forced upon him from outside. Democracy cannot be imposed upon a person; it has to be learned by a process of voluntary and responsible participation. Changing from autocracy to democracy is a process which takes more time than changing in the opposite direction.

3. The "learning" of democracy in case of a change from another pattern contains, therefore, a kind of paradox which is similar to the problem of leadership in democracy. The democratic leader does not impose his goals on the group as does the autocratic leader: the policy determination in democracy is done by the group as a whole. Still the democratic leader should "lead."

In regard to a change toward democracy this paradox of democratic leadership is still more pointed. In an experimental change, for instance, from individualistic freedom (laissez faire) to democracy, the incoming democratic leader could not tell the group members exactly what they should do because that would lead to autocracy. Still some manipulations of the situation had to be made to lead the group into the direction of democracy. A similarly difficult problem arose when the autocratic group was to be transformed into a democratic one. Relaxing the rules frequently led first to a period of aggressive anarchy.

To instigate changes toward democracy a situation has to be created for a certain period where the leader is sufficiently in control to rule out influences he does not want and to manipulate the situation to a sufficient degree. The goal of the democratic leader in this transition period will have to be the same as that of any good teacher, namely, to make himself superfluous, to be replaced by indigenous leaders from the group.

4. The experiments in training of democratic leaders, for instance, of foremen in a factory, indicate strongly that it does not suffice to have the subleaders who deal with the small face-to-face groups trained in democratic procedures. If the power above them, such as the management of the factory, does not understand and does not apply democratic procedures, either a revolution occurs or the effect of democratic leadership in the lower brackets will

quickly fade. This is not surprising because cultural patterns are social atmospheres which cannot be handed out bit by bit.

5. For reconstruction in European countries this means that it is a fallacy to believe that we can go on helping the Hapsburgs to set up an Austrian legion with the idea that "what government France, Germany, or the Balkan states will have will be decided not by us but by the people themselves after the war." Obviously, if we permit anti-democratic powers to establish themselves, people will have no chance to make a decision toward democracy.

Our task is to create that minimum degree of democracy which is necessary for an international organization of the type we wish to realize, that minimum which would permit us within a shrunken, interdependent world, to develop the democracy we want at home. For this purpose a political setting has to be provided which is powerful and enduring enough to give people at least a chance for "learning democracy."

To attack this problem realistically we will have to avoid an American imperialism which will police the world, as well as an American isolationism which will shy away from the responsibility required of any member of a democratic group of nations. We will have to avoid the naïve belief that people "left alone" will choose democracy. We have to avoid building our plans on "hatred of the enemy," but we also have to avoid building our plans on wishful thinking and blindness against reality. We should know, for instance, that we will have to deal in Germany with a set-up where month after month, day after day, six to seven thousand unwanted women and children are killed in central slaughter houses in occupied territories, and where thousands of people must have grown accustomed to doing such jobs. American newspapers seem to play down such unpleasant truths probably because they wish to prevent a peace based on hatred. Actually, this procedure defies its purpose because in politics as in education a successful action has to be based on a full knowledge of reality.

Considering the technical aspect of the change, one can state:

1. It is obviously hopeless to change the cultural patterns of millions of people by treating them individually. Fortunately, the

methods generally called "group work" permit reaching whole groups of individuals at once and, at the same time, seem actually to be more efficient in bringing about deep changes than the individual approach is.

2. It seems to be possible by training democratic leaders and leaders of leaders to build up a pyramid which could reach large masses relatively quickly.

3. It will be essential to have a set-up which avoids creating resentment and hostility and instead will build up co-operation. If one conceives the task of democratizing realistically as a process which has to reach deep into family action and everyday group life it seems to be somewhat hopeless to attempt such a change mainly through schools. Hundreds of thousands of American teachers would have to be sent over. These Americans, even hyphenated Americans and certainly refugees, are likely to create nothing but resentment in such a position.

There is, however, an historical precedent, at least in Germany, for Americans coming into the country with the purpose of helping on a wide scale and receiving enthusiastic support and acceptance by the Germans. The feeding of children throughout Germany after the last war, known in Germany as *"Quaekerspeisung"* (Quaker feeding), has left a deep impression in every German village and is remembered gratefully by millions of parents even now. It seems feasible and natural to build up group work around the feeding of Europe after this war in such a way that the co-operative work for reconstruction would offer a real experience in democratic group life. It would be possible to reach a large number and a variety of age levels in this and other works of reconstruction.

It is particularly important that in this way the adolescent could be reached. It is this age level which supports Hitler most uncritically and most unscrupulously. (For instance, the Super-Gestapo called Waffen-SS, whose function it would be to suppress any uprising in the army, is built from such young people.) In addition, the adolescent is at that age level which determines what the cultural pattern will be in the immediately following generation. The frontal attack on the task of transforming this very age level—which is full of enthusiasm and, in many respects, accustomed to co-operation—into co-operative groups for productive reconstruction in a radical democratic spirit might be one of the few chances for bringing about a change toward democracy which promises permanency.

3

THE SPECIAL CASE OF GERMANY

(1943)

BEFORE Pearl Harbor, in America probably more than in any other country, a fairly strong tendency was discernible to consider psychological factors such as frustration or "destructive traits" the basic cause for war. Accordingly, the avoidance of frustration was considered the main road to peace. Since then, a more realistic view of the importance of political and economic aspects seems to prevail. This shift of sentiment is to be welcomed, although there is now the danger that the pendulum will swing too far and that only the political aspects will be considered important. In planning the peace and in thinking of the future international conduct of other countries and of our own, we must realize also that the psychological and particularly the cultural factors are in the long run essential.

Thus it has been stated frequently that Hitlerism is but an extreme edition of that traditional militaristic Prussian culture which has governed Germany, to a considerable extent, since the founding of the Reich. It is not necessary to decide here whether or to what degree this is true. It would be more important to know in detail how deeply the Nazi culture is entrenched now within the various sections of the population. Although this question cannot fully be answered, at present, one can safely guess that Nazism is deeply rooted, particularly in the youth on whom the future depends. It is a culture which is centered around power as the supreme value and which denounces justice and equality of men again and again as the disgusting remnants of a decadent democracy.

The problem would be less severe if the ideals of egocentrism and ruthless power were limited to the conduct of war. The same values, unfortunately, have thoroughly penetrated all aspects of German culture including family life. Millions of helpless children, women, and men have been exterminated by suffocation or other means in the occupied countries during the last two years, and others are still killed daily. Tens of thousands of Germans must have become accustomed to serve as a matter of routine on the extermination squads or elsewhere in the large organization dedicated to this purpose. This systematic extermination has been carried out with the expressed purpose of securing in the generations to come German supremacy over the surrounding countries. For the question of international relations and of safeguarding the peace, it is particularly dangerous that such killing is considered the natural right of the victor over the vanquished or of the *Herrenvolk* over lower races.

Before discussing the problems of how a change might be accomplished, the objective should be clear. This objective cannot for Germany be a copy of the English or the American way of living. Whatever occurs, the resulting culture will be something specifically German. It will show the traces of its history and of the present extreme experiences of war and Nazism. This would hold true even if the new German culture should become thoroughly democratic.

There is one more reason to strive for a "democratic German" culture rather than an American or English culture. The limitation of the democratic principle of tolerance toward others is defined by the maxim of "democratic intolerance toward intolerance." This right and duty to intolerance is very important if democracy is to live anywhere on this globe. This principle does not, however, demand conformity; it limits our rightful interest to certain minimum requirements which are probably not too different from the minimum requirements for international peace.

CULTURAL CHANGES OF INDIVIDUALS AND NATIONS

Even formulated in this way, a change toward democratic German culture obviously includes very difficult problems.

There is no question but that the culture of individuals or small groups can be changed deeply in a relatively short time. A child transplanted from Germany or Japan to America will, as a rule, become thoroughly Americanized. Even grown-ups who are transplanted to a different culture may acquire the new culture to a high degree, and much can be done toward this end through proper education. Experiments with both children and adults prove that the social atmosphere of groups can be changed profoundly by introducing different forms of leadership. Experiments in leadership training have shown that it is even possible under certain circumstances to transform highly autocratic leaders of long standing within a short time into efficient democratic leaders.

All of these changes, however, are changes of individuals or small groups in a direction which is in line with some aspects of the general cultural setting in which these individuals or groups live. To change the culture of a whole nation is quite a different undertaking. The greater numbers involved present merely one of the difficulties. Even more important are certain dynamic relations between the various aspects of the culture of a nation—such as its education, mores, political behavior, religious outlook—which interact in a way that tends to bend any deviation from the established culture back to the same old stream.

There is no space here to discuss these dynamics in detail. I might merely remind the reader that the difference, for instance, between the American and the German culture is discernible more or less in every part of their respective cultural lives: in the way the mother treats a two- or three-year-old child, what the father talks about at the dinner table, how the worker talks to his foreman or the student to the professor, how the visitor behaves toward grown-ups and children, how the cookbooks are written, how opposing lawyers deal with each other after the court session, what type of photograph the candidate for political office uses for propaganda, and what religion means to a person in any denomination. A cultural change in regard to a specific item will have to be able to stand up against the weight of the thousand and one items of the rest of the culture which tend to turn the conduct back to its old pattern. As someone has put it, "Cultures are pretty watertight."

We may conclude: To be stable, a cultural change has to penetrate more or less into all aspects of a nation's life. The change must, in short, be a change in the "cultural atmosphere," not merely a change of single items.

GENERAL ASPECTS OF CULTURAL CHANGE

1. *Culture as an equilibrium.* A culture is not a painted picture; it is a living process, composed of countless social interactions. Like a river whose form and velocity are determined by the balance of those forces that tend to make the water flow faster, and the friction that tends to make the water flow more slowly—the cultural pattern of a people at a given time is maintained by a balance of counteracting forces. The study of cultures on a smaller scale indicates that, for instance, the speed of production or other aspects of the atmosphere of a factory has to be understood as an equilibrium, or more precisely, as an "equilibrium in movement."

Once a given level is established, certain self-regulatory processes come into function which tend to keep group life on that level. One speaks of "work habits," "established customs," the "accepted way of doing things." Special occasions may bring about a momentary rise of production, a festival may create for a day or two a different social atmosphere between management and workers, but quickly the effect of the "shot in the arm" will fade out and the basic constellation of forces will re-establish the old forms of everyday living.

The general problem, therefore, of changing the social atmosphere of a factory or of German culture can be formulated somewhat more precisely in this way: How can a situation be brought about which would permanently change the level on which the counteracting forces find their quasi-stationary equilibrium?

2. *Changing the constellation of forces.* To bring about any change, the balance between the forces which maintain the social self-regulation at a given level has to be upset.

This implies for Germany that certain deep-seated powers have to be uprooted. Large proportions of those sections of the German population on which a democratic reconstruction will depend live now in a state of suppression and terror. It is hardly conceivable that these people will be able to act freely as long as they see the Gestapo or other masters of ten years of terror alive and free on the other side of the street. After the last war the reactionary forces in Germany, although driven under cover, were permitted to "get away with it." Being a socially well-knit group, they soon started to come back step by step and to take their revenge in the extreme form of Hitlerism. I cannot see any hope of more than superficial change after the present war if the German people are prevented from getting rid in a very thorough fashion of a large group which has developed to perfection the most ruthless methods of suppression. This group, at present, is known to be already preparing to go underground; it will remain a powerful threat if its utter destruction is hindered by forces outside Germany fearing any type of "chaos."

The German move toward democracy after the last war did not fail because the so-called German Revolution of 1918 was too chaotic, but because the overthrow of the Kaiser was entirely bloodless and did not reach deep enough. It did not reach deep enough socially to remove certain sections of the population from power, and it did not reach deep enough culturally to remove the idea of democracy from its identification with individualistic freedom of the laissez faire type. A revolution in Germany should, therefore, be viewed as a positive factor, not a negative one, in bringing about the desired end—a move toward democracy and permanent peace.

3. *Establishing a new cultural pattern.* Hand in hand with the destruction of the forces maintaining the old equilibrium must go the establishment (or liberation) of forces toward a new equilibrium. Not only is it essential to create the fluidity necessary for

change and to effect the change itself; it is also imperative that steps be taken to bring about the permanence of the new situation through self-regulation on the new level.

TECHNIQUES OF CHANGING CULTURE

Let us assume that the situation in Germany will be sufficiently fluid. Is there anything that can be done to help the forces which may establish a new level of equilibrium closer to democracy? From the many considerations, I shall mention but a few.

1. *"Satisfaction" is not enough.* If the many needs of the German people are satisfied, will that not suffice to make them democratic? This idea, rather common before America's entrance into the war, may well be brought to life again as soon as the war with Germany is over (although it will hardly be propagated in this country in regard to the Japanese). Such suggestions are based on the naïve idea that "human nature" is identical with "democratic culture"; that one needs but to destroy the causes of maladjustment to create a democratic world.

I had a chance to observe rather closely a young fellow who had been active in the German Youth movement before Hitler. Subsequently he had been taken over by the Nazis and made an assistant to a District Youth leader for a number of years. For one reason or another he had fled the country and become politically anti-Nazi. This individual showed rather marked symptoms of maladjustment such as aggressiveness and egocentricism. Being a clever fellow, he made his way, learned the amenities of the American style, and showed a friendly and smooth surface. After a number of years he gave the appearance of being quite well adjusted and was usually considered a likeable fellow.

Only those who knew him intimately and followed his actions closely for a long time could see that actually his conduct has become more insidious than ever before. Having an exceptionally fine sense for relations of status and power, the fellow would find out immediately who were friends, who enemies, where lay the strength or weakness of everyone, or what ideas were fashionable at the moment. On the basis of this quickly gained intimate knowledge of power relations he would pursue an active, egoistic policy with an extreme degree of aggressiveness, using lies without inhibition and figuring out destructive frontal attacks with a cleverness that made people gasp. I could not help but feel that here we had a practically "pure" case of Nazi culture. This aggressiveness did not diminish but rather increased and became more dangerous as the individual became personally secure without changing his basic culture.

I think this is a clear example of the fact that, in an aggressive autocratic culture, aggression and autocratic behavior cannot be viewed as symptoms of maladjustment. They cannot be basically changed merely by satisfying the individual's need.

2. *Some general positive principles.* The studies of group life in various fields suggest a few general principles for changing group culture.

(a) The change has to be a change of group atmosphere rather than of single items. We have discussed this problem already. Technically it means that the change cannot be accomplished by learning tricks. It must be deeper than the verbal level or the level of social or legal formalities.

(b) It can be shown that the system of values which governs the ideology of a group is dynamically linked with other power aspects within the life of the group. This is correct psychologically as well as historically. Any real change of the culture of a group is, therefore, interwoven with the changes of power constellation within the group.

(c) From this point it will be easily understood why a change in methods of leadership is probably the quickest way to bring about a change in the cultural atmosphere of a group. For the status and power of the leader or of the leading section of a group make them the key to the ideology and the organization of the life of that group.

3. *The change from autocracy to democracy.* Experiments on groups and leadership training suggest the following conclusions:

(a) The change of a group atmosphere from autocracy or laissez faire to democracy through a democratic leader amounts to a re-education of the followers toward "democratic followership." Any group atmosphere can be conceived of as a pattern of role playing. Neither the autocratic nor the democratic leader can play his role without the followers being ready to play their role accordingly. Without the members of the group being able and ready to take over those responsibilities which are essential for follower-ships in a democracy, the democratic leader will be helpless. Changing a group atmosphere from autocracy toward democracy through a democratic leadership, therefore, means that the autocratic followers must shift toward a genuine acceptance of the role of democratic followers.

(b) The experiments show that this shift in roles cannot be accomplished by a "hands off" policy. To apply the principle of "individualistic freedom" merely leads to chaos. Sometimes people must rather forcefully be made to see what democratic responsibility toward the group as a whole means. It is true that people cannot be trained for democracy by autocratic methods. But it is equally true that to be able to change a group atmosphere toward democracy the democratic leader has to be in power and has to use his power for active re-education. There is no space here to discuss in detail what to some might appear as one of the paradoxes of democracy. The more the group members become converted to democracy and learn to play the roles of democracy as followers or leaders, the more can the power of the democratic leader shift to other ends than converting the group members.

(c) From what has been said up to now it should be clear that lecture and propaganda do not suffice to bring about the necessary change. Essential as they are, they will be effective only if combined with a change in the power relations and leadership of the group. For larger groups, this means that a hierarchy of leaders has to be trained which reaches out into all essential sub-parts of the group. Hitler himself has obviously followed very carefully such a procedure. The democratic reversal of this procedure, although different in many respects, will have to be as thorough and as solidly based on group organization.

(d) By and large the same principle holds for the training of democratic leaders as for the training of the other members of the group. Democratic leaders cannot be trained autocratically; it is, on the other hand, of utmost importance that the trainer of democratic leaders establish and hold his position of leadership. It is, furthermore, very important that the people who are to be changed from another atmosphere toward democracy be dissatisfied with the previous situation and feel the need for a change. There are indications that it is easier to change an unsatisfied autocratic leader toward democratic techniques than to change a laissez faire type of leader or a satisfied half-democratic leader. This may be contrary to the popular notion that a change is the more easily accomplished the greater the similarity between the beginning and the end situation. From the general theory of cultural change it is, however, understandable why after small changes the tendency to return to the previous level of equilibrium might be stronger than after great changes.

THE HEART OF THE GERMAN PROBLEM

It seems to follow, then, that the basic requirement of a change in German culture toward democracy is a change in the role of the leaders and of the followers.

That German citizens have never known how to criticize their bosses has frequently been observed. In German culture "loyalty" is typically identified with "obedience." They do not see any other alternative to efficient group organization based on obedience but an atmosphere of laissez faire and inefficiency based on individualistic freedom. The Hitler regime has done everything to strengthen this view and to identify democracy with decadent inefficient lawlessness. After the last war the liberal German newspapers discussed the meaning of democratic leadership and democratic discipline in an attempt to educate the public away from the alternative of blind obedience or respectlessness and lack of responsibility. The English idea of "His Majesty's loyal opposition" was used to point out the positive functions and the responsibilities which the opposition parties have in a parliamentary system. To the German reader these articles sounded strangely unreal and unbelievable. They seemed as contrary to the German concept of human nature as the idea of fair play, a concept utterly strange to German culture.

Such articles, obviously, had little influence on the political action of the Germans; I doubt whether the results would have been better if they had been multiplied a hundredfold. To understand what is being talked about the individual has to have a basis in experience—as a child in a student council, in the hundred and one associations of everyday life; he has to have some taste of what democratic leadership and the democratic responsibility of the follower mean. No lecture can substitute for these first-hand experiences.

Only through practical experience can one learn that peculiar democratic combination of conduct which includes responsibility toward the group, ability to recognize differences of opinion without considering the other person a criminal, and readiness to accept criticism in a matter of fact way while offering criticism with sensitivity for the other person's feeling. The attempt to change one element alone will merely lead to a situation where the weight of the other elements will re-establish the previous total pattern.

WHO CAN BE CHANGED IN GERMANY?

Which groups of people are particularly important for the positive aspects of reconstruction?

In regard to social classes, we have already discussed the necessity for breaking the rule of the Gestapo and the Junkers. It is difficult, without knowing in detail the present social constellation, to make any definite statement. As we have seen, a strong change in the cultural setting has more chance of permanence than a slight one (although there is, of course, the phenomenon of the pendulum's swinging too far). It would be most unfortunate if the attempt were made to place in power those sections of the German population whose aim it is merely to return to the pre-Hitler atmosphere in Germany and who are afraid of any drastic democratic setting. Such a situation—for instance, the establishment of the Hapsburgs in Austria—would not be stable; it would either mean the return to Fascism in a modified form or—and that is more likely—it would lead to a genuine revolutionary uprising.

More than usual one will have to take the age levels into consideration. In regard to changes, three age levels might be distinguished: (a) the people above forty who have experienced something other than Nazism in their mature lives; (b) the people between twenty and thirty whose formative years have been dominated by Fascism and who are thoroughly indoctrinated; and (c) the children. For each group the problem is somewhat different. We shall discuss briefly the first and the second, because they will determine the atmosphere in which the children will be acculturated.

(1) Among the people over forty there are many who had strong liberal convictions. Although most of the leftist leaders may have been killed, there is doubtless a sizable body of people who are ready and eager to establish a new "free" Germany. We might expect that many will have learned from the mistakes after 1918 and will try to do a better job this time. Along cultural lines these people probably need most a better understanding of how an efficient democracy works. What they at present understand as democracy or freedom lacks both the leadership and the discipline of an efficient democracy.

(2) The twenty-year-olds who have no cultural past other than Fascism to which they could return and who have well-established cultural habits are considered by some observers as a "lost generation." They might well become that, go underground, and prepare the next world war; for that seems the only ideal toward which a generation in whom Nazi culture remains shaken but not changed can strive.

I am not persuaded, however, that this is the only possibility. A large section of this group must now be inwardly desperate. They know that something is wrong with Nazism. It would not be surprising, therefore, if this group were psychologically in a frame of mind not so different from the psychological situation of the autocratic leaders in the experiments—the ones who were "converted" and retrained in a short time. It seems not at all impossible that a frontal attack on the problem of changing a selected group of young Nazi leaders in every field of endeavor would be more successful in bringing about a radical change from autocracy toward democracy in Germany than the attempt to remodel the older generation whose ideal leaned toward laissez faire. These young people who are familiar with problems of leadership and who have a deep need for change would—if they could be changed —promise a more deep and stable change in atmosphere than groups that strive toward a return to the old or toward slight changes. There is, of course, no hope for conversion of the young without a strong and new positive ideal.

WAYS OF CHANGING GERMAN CULTURE

Mere propaganda, and particularly propaganda from the outside, will not change German culture. If a sufficiently deep and permanent change is to be accomplished, the individual will have to be approached in his capacity as a member of groups. It is as a member of a group that the individual is most pliable. At the same time such a group approach can better influence relatively deeply large masses than either the individual approach or the mass approach through propaganda.

It is natural to think of the school system—from the nursery school to the university—as an organization through which the culture of a nation can be changed. Yet one should be clear about its limitations. The idea, for example, of using some 100,000 for-eign teachers or former refugees seems to have been abandoned, because it would lead to nothing but a strong negative reaction. It has been suggested, again, that the Allies be content with securing certain minimum requirements concerning textbooks; that, of course, would not contribute much toward changing German culture.

I think one should neither under- nor over-rate the importance of the educational system. It is, of course, very important for long-range planning. Yet the atmosphere in education is but a mirror and an expression of the culture of the country; it changes with every change of its general social atmosphere—as the history of

German education between 1918 and 1933 shows strikingly enough. Education of children, therefore, is in the beginning less important than a change in leadership.

Change in culture requires the change of leadership forms in every walk of life. At the start, particularly important is leadership in those social areas which are fundamental from the point of view of power. Ideology and power problems are closely linked. *The shift of political power to other sections of the population and the change in leadership techniques in the fields of politics, law, law enforcement, and economics are, therefore, fundamental. Only as a part of such a political change can a cultural change toward democracy occur and survive.*

To my mind, not too much can be expected from an exchange of potential leaders between countries, although such an undertaking is laudable. There is a definite limit to what a person can learn in the unrealistic setting of being a guest, outside of the particular atmosphere in which he will have to work. Much more promising would be a training "on the job." The reconstruction after the war should provide ample possibilities of collaboration for Germans and non-Germans, opportunities which could well be used for the training or retraining of youthful German leaders. This training does not need to bear the stigma of "education," because a job is to be done, a job of co-operation in the interest of Germany. It could be demonstrated there and experienced firsthand that "democracy works better." If strategically managed, such training on the job of leaders and trainers of leaders might well reach into every aspect of community leadership. It might help to set in motion a process of self-re-education.

The ideas discussed herein seem to point to a procedure which offers at least some realistic hope of success. Whether or not an attempt along this line can be made, and how successful it would be, depends on the world situation. Moses led Israel through the desert for forty years, until the generation that had lived as slaves might die, and the rest learn to live as free people. Perhaps there are still no faster or better methods for the permanent cultural re-education of a nation.

4

CONDUCT, KNOWLEDGE, AND ACCEPTANCE OF NEW VALUES[1]

(1945)

WHAT is the nature of the re-educative process? What causes it to "take"? What are the resistances likely to be encountered? The need for re-education arises when an individual or group is out of step with society at large. If the individual has taken to alcoholism, for instance, or has become a criminal, the process of re-education attempts to lead him back to the values and conduct which are in tune with the society in which he lives.

The definition of the purpose of re-education could stop here if society as a whole were always in line with reality. Since this is not the case, we have to add: Re-education is needed also when an individual or group is out of touch with reality. We are dealing with what might be described as a divergence from the norm or from the reality of objective facts. The question which we have to ask in considering the problem is this: What has to happen in the individual in order that he give up the divergence and become reoriented toward a norm, or, as the case may be, toward a closer contact with reality?

THE ORIGIN OF A DIVERGENCE

Social scientists agree that differences in conduct as they exist today among men, white, black, or yellow, are not innate; they are

---

[1] The material in this chapter was prepared jointly by Dr. Lewin and Mr. Paul Grabbe.

acquired. Divergences from the social norm are also acquired. Efforts to find an explanation of such divergences in "basic personality differences" have been unrewarding. It is probably correct to formulate the following, more precise hypothesis:

1. *The processes governing the acquisition of the normal and abnormal are fundamentally alike.*

The nature of the processes by which the individual becomes a criminal, for instance, seems to be basically the same as the processes by which the nondiverging individual is led to conduct which is considered honest. What counts is the effect upon the individual of the circumstances of his life, the influence of the group in which he has grown up. The normality of this influence is stressed with reference to the alcoholic and delinquent and holds apparently for many other types of divergences from the social norm: the prostitute, for instance, or even the autocrat.

The same undoubtedly is true of those divergences in which beliefs and conduct run counter to reality. The processes which give rise to them—a super-patriot's belief, for instance, that all "foreigners" are "reds"—are fundamentally the same in nature as those by which this individual acquires a sufficiently realistic view of family and friends to get along in the community. His wrong stereotype about foreigners is a form of social illusion. To understand its origin, let us note a conclusion reached by psychologists in the field of space perception: that the processes responsible for the creation of "inadequate" visual images (illusions) and those which give rise to "adequate" visual images ("reality") are identical in nature.

Experiments dealing with memory and group pressure on the individual show that what exists as "reality" for the individual is, to a high degree, determined by what is socially accepted as reality. This holds even in the field of physical fact: to the South Sea Islander the world may be flat; to the European, it is round. "Reality," therefore, is not an absolute. It differs with the group to which the individual belongs.

This dependence of the individual on the group for a determination of what does and what does not constitute "reality" is less surprising if we remember that the individual's own experience is necessarily limited. In other words, the probability that his judgment will be right is heightened if the individual places greater trust in the experience of the group, whether or not this group experience tallies with his own. This is one reason for the acceptance of the group's judgment, but there is still another reason. In any field of conduct and beliefs, the group exercises strong pressure for compliance on its individual members. We are subject to this pressure in all areas—political, religious, social—including our beliefs of what is true or false, good or bad, right or wrong, real or unreal.

Under these circumstances it is not difficult to understand why the general acceptance of a fact or a belief might be the very cause preventing this belief or fact from ever being questioned.

RE-EDUCATION AS A CHANGE IN CULTURE

If the processes which lead to prejudices and illusions, and those which lead to correct perception and realistic social concepts are essentially the same, then re-education must be a process that is functionally similar to a change in culture. It is a process in which changes of knowledge and beliefs, changes of values and standards, changes of emotional attachments and needs, and changes of everyday conduct occur not piecemeal and independently of each other, but within the framework of the individual's total life in the group.

From this viewpoint, even the re-education of a carpenter who is to become a watchmaker is not merely a matter of teaching the carpenter a set of new watchmaking skills. Before he can become a watchmaker, the carpenter, in addition to the learning of a set of new skills, will have to acquire a new system of habits, standards, and values—the standards and values which characterize the thinking and behavior of watchmakers. At least, this is what he will have to do before he can function successfully as a watchmaker.

Re-education in this sense is equivalent to the process by which the individual, in growing into the culture in which he finds himself, acquires the system of values and the set of facts which later come to govern his thinking and conduct. Accordingly, it would appear that

2. The re-educative process has to fulfill a task which is essentially equivalent to a change in culture.

We can now more easily understand why "informality of education" is stressed as such an important factor in the re-education of the delinquent; why the all-inclusive atmosphere characteristic of life in and with a group like Alcoholics Anonymous is said to be so much more effective in helping the drinker to give up alcohol than the long and exacting routine of specific habit training which the alcoholic has to undergo as a medical patient.

Only by anchoring his own conduct in something as large, substantial, and superindividual as the culture of a group can the individual stabilize his new beliefs sufficiently to keep them immune from the day-by-day fluctuations of moods and influences to which he, as an individual, is subject.

To view re-education as a task of acculturation is, we think, a basic and worth-while insight. However, it is but a frame of reference. To provide for effective re-education, we need additional insight into the dynamics of the process, the specific constellation of forces which have to be dealt with under varying conditions.

INNER CONTRADICTIONS IN RE-EDUCATION

The re-educative process affects the individual in three ways. It changes his *cognitive structure*, the way he sees the physical and social worlds, including all his facts, concepts, beliefs, and expectations. It modifies his *valences and values*, and these embrace both his attractions and aversions to groups and group standards, his feelings in regard to status differences, and his reactions to sources of approval or disapproval. And it affects *motoric action*, involving the degree of the individual's control over his physical and social movements.

If all three of these effects (and the processes which give rise to them) were governed by the same laws, the practical task of re-education would be much simpler. Unfortunately they are not, and the re-educator, in consequence, is confronted with certain contradictions. For instance, treatment involving the training of a thumb-sucking child in certain roundabout hand movements, designed to make the child aware of his thumb-sucking and thereby giving him more control over these movements, may set the child apart from other children and undermine his emotional security, the possession of which is a prerequisite for successful re-education.

How these inner contradictions may be avoided is one of the basic problems of re-education. A correct sequence of steps, correct timing, and a correct combination of individual and group treatments are presumably essential. Most important, however, is a thorough understanding by the re-educator of the way in which each of these psychological components—the *cognitive structure*, *valences and values*, and *motoric action*—are affected by any specific step in re-education.

The discussion that follows touches but two of the main problems here involved, one related to a change in cognition, the other, to the acceptance of new values.

CHANGE IN THE COGNITIVE STRUCTURE

The difficulties encountered in efforts to reduce prejudices or otherwise to change the social outlook of the individual have led to a realization that re-education cannot be merely a rational process. We know that lectures or other similarly abstract methods of transmitting knowledge are of little avail in changing his subsequent outlook and conduct. We might be tempted, therefore, to think that what is lacking in these methods is first-hand experience. The sad truth is that even first-hand experience will not necessarily produce the desired result. To understand the reasons, we must examine a number of premises which bear directly on the problem.

3. *Even extensive first-hand experience does not automatically create correct concepts (knowledge).*

For thousands of years man's everyday experience with falling objects did not suffice to bring him to a correct theory of gravity. A sequence of very unusual, man-made experiences, so-called experiments, which grew out of the systematic search for the truth were necessary to bring about a change from less adequate to more adequate concepts. To assume that first-hand experience in the social world would automatically lead to the formation of correct concepts or to the creation of adequate stereotypes seems therefore unjustifiable.

4. Social action no less than physical action is steered by perception.

In any situation we cannot help but act according to the field we perceive; and our perception extends to two different aspects of this field. One has to do with facts, the other with values.

If we grasp an object, the movement of our hand is steered by its perceived position in the perceived surroundings. Likewise, our social actions are steered by the position in which we perceive ourselves and others within the total social setting. The basic task of re-education can thus be viewed as one of changing the individual's social perception. Only by this change in social perception can change in the individual's social action be realized.

Let us assume that inadequate information (knowledge) has somehow been replaced by more adequate knowledge. Does this suffice to change our perception? In answering this question, let us again take a lead from the field of physical perception by asking: How can false physical perception, for instance, visual illusions, be rectified?

5. As a rule, the possession of correct knowledge does not suffice to rectify false perception.

Our insight into the conditions which determine the correctness or incorrectness of perception is still very limited. It is known that some relation exists between visual perception and knowledge. However, the lines which appear curved in an optical illusion do not straighten out as soon as we "know" that they are straight. Even first-hand experience, the measuring of the distances in question, usually does not eliminate the illusion. As a rule, other types of change, such as the enlarging or the shrinking of the area perceived or a change in the visual frames of references are needed to straighten out the lines.

When we consider resistances to re-education we usually think in terms of emotional obstacles. It is important, however, not to underestimate the difficulties inherent in changing cognition. If we keep in mind that even extensive experience with physical facts does not necessarily lead to correct physical perception, we will be less surprised at the resistances encountered when we attempt to modify inadequate social stereotypes.

French and Marrow tell the story of a forelady's attitude toward older workers. She clings to the conviction that older workers are no good, although she has older workers on her floor whom she considers very efficient. Her prejudices stand in direct opposition to all her personal experience.

This example from industry is well in line with studies on Negro-White relations dealing with the effect of common schooling and with observations on the effect of mingling. They indicate that favorable experiences with members of another group, even if they are frequent, do not necessarily diminish prejudices toward that group.

Only if a psychological linkage is made between the image of specific individuals and the stereotype of a certain group, only when the individuals can be perceived as "typical representatives" of that group, is the experience with individuals likely to affect the stereotype.

6. Incorrect stereotypes (prejudices) are functionally equivalent to wrong concepts (theories).

We can infer, for instance, that the social experiences which are needed to change improper stereotypes have to be equivalent to those rare and specific physical experiences which cause a change in our theories and concepts about the physical world. Such experiences cannot be depended on to happen accidentally.

To understand the difficulties in the way of changing conduct, an additional point has to be considered:

7. Changes in sentiments do not necessarily follow changes in cognitive structure.

Even if the cognitive structure in regard to a group is modified in an individual, his sentiments toward this group may remain unchanged. The analysis of an opinion survey on the Negro problem, involving white respondents with varying educational backgrounds, shows that knowledge and sentiment are independent to a marked degree.

The sentiments of the individual toward a group are determined less by his knowledge about that group than by the sentiments prevalent in the social atmosphere which surrounds him. Just as the alcoholic knows that he should not drink—and doesn't want to drink; so the white American soldier who observes a Negro dating a white girl in England may feel that he should not mind—and he might consciously condemn himself for his prejudices. Still he may frequently be helpless in the face of this prejudice since his perception and emotional reaction remain contrary to what he knows they ought to be.

Re-education is frequently in danger of reaching only the official system of values, the level of verbal expression and not of conduct; it may result in merely heightening the discrepancy between the super-ego (the way I ought to feel) and the ego (the way I really feel), and thus give the individual a bad conscience. Such a discrepancy leads to a state of high emotional tension but seldom to correct conduct. It may postpone transgressions but is likely to make transgressions more violent when they occur.

A factor of great importance in bringing about a change in sentiment is the degree to which the individual becomes actively involved in the problem. Lacking this involvement, no objective fact is likely to reach the status of a fact for the individual concerned and therefore influence his social conduct.

The nature of this interdependence becomes somewhat more understandable if one considers the relation between change in perception, acceptance, and group belongingness.

ACCEPTANCE OF NEW VALUES AND GROUP BELONGINGNESS

Since action is ruled by perception, a change in conduct presupposes that new facts and values are perceived. These have to be accepted not merely verbally as an official ideology, but as an action-ideology, involving that particular, frequently non-conscious, system of values which guides conduct. In other words,

8. *A change in action-ideology, a real acceptance of a changed set of. facts and values, a change in the perceived social world—all three are but different expressions of the same process.*

By some, this process may be called a change in the culture of the individual; by others, a change of his super-ego.

It is important to note that re-education will be successful, i.e., lead to permanent change, only if this change in culture is sufficiently complete. If re-education succeeds only to the degree that the individual becomes a marginal man between the old and new system of values, nothing worth while is accomplished.

One of the factors which has been shown to have a very important bearing on the success or failure of the re-educative process is the manner in which the new super-ego is introduced. The simplest solution seems to lie in outright enforcement of the new set of values and beliefs. In this case a new god is introduced who has to fight with the old god, now regarded as a devil. Two points may be made in this connection, illustrating the dilemma facing re-education in regard to the introduction of a new set of values.

a. Loyalty to the old and hostility to the new values. An individual who is forcibly moved from his own to another country, with a different culture, is likely to meet the new set of values with hostility. So it is with an individual who is made a subject of re-education against his will. Feeling threatened, he reacts with hostility. This threat is felt all the more keenly if the individual is not voluntarily exposing himself to re-education. A comparison of voluntary and involuntary migration from one culture to another seems to bear out this observation.

One would expect this hostility to be the more pronounced the greater the loyalty of the individual to the old system of values. Accordingly, persons who are more socially inclined, therefore less self-centered, can be expected to offer stronger resistances to re-education, for the very reason that they are more firmly anchored in the old system.

In any event, the re-educative process will normally encounter hostility. The task of breaking down this hostility becomes a paradox if one considers the relation between acceptance of new values and freedom of choice.

b. Re-education and freedom of acceptance. Much stress is laid on the creation, as part of the re-educative process, of an atmosphere of freedom and spontaneity. Voluntary attendance, informality of meetings, freedom of expression in voicing grievances, emotional security, and avoidance of pressure, all include this element. Carl Rogers' emphasis on self-decision by the patient stresses the same point for the psychotherapy of the individual.

There seems to be a paradox implied in this insistence on freedom of acceptance, and probably no other aspect of re-education brings more clearly into the open a basic difficulty of the process. Since re-education aims to change the system of values and beliefs of an individual or a group, to change it so as to bring it in line with society at large or with reality, it seems illogical to expect that this change will be made by the subjects themselves. The fact that this change has to be enforced on the individual from outside seems so obvious a necessity that it is often taken for granted. Many people assume that the creation, as part of the re-educative process, of an atmosphere of informality and freedom of choice cannot possibly mean anything else but that the re-educator must be clever enough in manipulating the subjects to have them think that they are running the show. According to such people, an approach of this kind is merely a deception and smoke-screen for what to them is the more honorable, straightforward method of using force.

It may be pointed out, however, that if re-education means the establishment of a new super-ego, it necessarily follows that the objective sought will not be reached so long as the new set of values is not experienced by the individual as something freely chosen. If the individual complies merely from fear of punishment rather than through the dictates of his free will and conscience, the new set of values he is expected to accept does not assume in him the position of super-ego, and his re-education therefore remains unrealized.

From this we may conclude that social perception and freedom of choice are interrelated. Following one's conscience is identical with following the perceived intrinsic requirements of the situation. Only if and when the new set of values is freely accepted, only if it corresponds to one's super-ego, do those changes in social perception occur which, as we have seen, are a prerequisite for a change in conduct and therefore for a lasting effect of re-education.

We can now formulate the dilemma which re-education has to face in this way: How can free acceptance of a new system of values be brought about if the person who is to be educated is, in the nature of things, likely to be hostile to the new values and loyal to the old?

9. *Acceptance of the new set of values and beliefs cannot usually be brought about item by item.*

Methods and procedures which seek to change convictions item by item are of little avail in bringing about the desired change of heart. This is found to be one of the most important experiences for those engaged in the field of re-education. Arguments proceeding logically from one point to another may drive the individual into a corner. But as a rule he will find some way—if necessary a very illogical way—to retain his beliefs. No change of conviction on any specific point can be established in more than an ephemeral way so long as the individual has not given up his hostility to the new set of values as a whole, to the extent of having changed from hostility at least to open-mindedness.

Step-by-step methods *are* very important in re-education. These steps, however, have to be conceived as steps in a gradual change from hostility to friendliness in regard to the new system as a whole rather than as a conversion of the individual one point at a time. Of course, convictions in regard to certain points in the total system may play an important role in the process of conversion. It is, however, important for the over-all planning of re-education not to lose sight of the fact that efforts directed toward bringing about a change from hostility to open-mindedness and to friendliness to the new culture as a whole be given priority over conversion in regard to any single item or series of items of the re-educative program.

How, then, can acceptance of the new values be established if not by an item-by-item change in conviction?

CREATION OF AN IN-GROUP AND THE ACCEPTANCE OF A NEW VALUE SYSTEM

One of the outstanding means used today for bringing about acceptance in re-education, as discussed above, is the establishment of what is called an "in-group," i.e., a group in which the members feel belongingness. Under these circumstances,

10. *The individual accepts the new system of values and beliefs by accepting belongingness to a group.*

Allport formulates this point as a general principle of teaching people when he says, "It is an axiom that people cannot be taught who feel that they are at the same time being attacked." The normal gap between teacher and student, doctor and patient, social worker and public, can, therefore, be a real obstacle to acceptance of the advocated conduct. In other words, in spite of whatever status differences there might be between them, the teacher and the student have to feel as members of one group in matters involving their sense of values.

The chances for re-education seem to be increased whenever a strong we-feeling is created. The establishment of this feeling that everybody is in the same boat, has gone through the same difficulties, and speaks the same language is stressed as one of the main conditions facilitating the re-education of the alcoholic and the delinquent.

When re-education involves the relinquishment of standards which are contrary to the standards of society at large (as in the case of delinquency, minority prejudices, alcoholism), the feeling of group belongingness seems to be greatly heightened if the members feel free to express openly the very sentiments which are to be dislodged through re-education. This might be viewed as another example of the seeming contradictions inherent in the process of re-education: Expression of prejudices against minorities or the breaking of rules of parliamentary procedures may in themselves be contrary to the desired goal. Yet a feeling of complete freedom and a heightened group identification are frequently more important at a particular stage of re-education than learning not to break specific rules.

This principle of in-grouping makes understandable why complete acceptance of previously rejected facts can be achieved best through the discovery of these facts by the group members themselves. Then, and frequently only then, do the facts become really *their* facts (as against other people's facts). An individual will believe facts he himself has discovered in the same way that he believes in himself or in his group. The importance of this fact-finding process for the group by the group itself has been recently emphasized with reference to re-education in several fields. It can be surmised that the extent to which social research is translated into social action depends on the degree to which those who carry out this action are made a part of the fact-finding on which the action is to be based.

Re-education influences conduct only when the new system of values and beliefs dominates the individual's perception. The acceptance of the new system is linked with the acceptance of a specific group, a particular role, a definite source of authority as new points of reference. It is basic for re-education that this linkage between acceptance of new facts or values and acceptance of certain groups or roles is very intimate and that the second frequently is a prerequisite for the first. This explains the great difficulty of changing beliefs and values in a piecemeal fashion. This linkage is a main factor behind resistance to re-education, but can also be made a powerful means for successful re-education.

Part II. CONFLICTS IN FACE-TO-FACE GROUPS

5

EXPERIMENTS IN SOCIAL SPACE

(1939)

I.

I AM PERSUADED that it is possible to undertake experiments in sociology which have as much right to be called scientific experiments as those in physics and chemistry. I am persuaded that there exists a social space which has all the essential properties of a real empirical space and deserves as much attention by students of geometry and mathematics as the physical space, although it is *not* a physical one. The perception of social space and the experimental and conceptual investigation of the dynamics and laws of the processes in social space are of fundamental theoretical and practical importance.

Being officially a psychologist I should perhaps apologize to the sociologists for crossing the boundaries of my field. My justification for doing so is that necessity forces the move, and for this the sociologists themselves are partially to blame. For they have stressed that the view which holds a human being to be a biological, physiological entity is utterly wrong. They have fought against the belief that only physical or biological facts are real, and that social facts are merely an abstraction. Some of the sociologists have said that only the social group has reality and that the individual person is nothing more than an abstraction—a being who properly should be described as a cross section of the groups to which he belongs.

Whichever of these statements one might consider correct,

one certainly will have to admit that psychology has learned, particularly in the last decade, to realize the overwhelming importance of social factors for practically every kind and type of behavior. It is true that the child from the first day of his life is a member of a group and would die without being cared for by the group. The experiments on success and failure, level of aspiration, intelligence, frustration, and all the others, have shown more and more convincingly that the goal a person sets for himself is deeply influenced by the social standards of the group to which he belongs or wishes to belong. The psychologist of today recognizes that there are few problems more important for the development of the child and the problem of adolescence than a study of the processes by which a child takes over or becomes opposed to the ideology and the style of living predominant in his social climate, the forces which make him belong to certain groups, or which determine his social status and his security within those groups.

A genuine attempt to approach these problems experimentally —for instance, that of social status or leadership—implies technically that one has to create different types of groups and to set up experimentally a variety of social factors which might shift this status. The experimental social psychologist will have to acquaint himself with the task of experimentally creating groups, creating a social climate or style of living. The sociologist I hope will therefore forgive him when he cannot avoid handling also the so-called sociological problems of groups and group life. Perhaps the social psychologist might prove to be even of considerable help to the sociologist. Frequently the investigation on the border line between two sciences has proved to be particularly fruitful for the progress of both of them.

Take, for instance, the concept "social group." There has been much discussion about how to define a group. The group often has been considered as something more than the sum of the individuals, something better and higher. One has attributed to it a "group mind." The opponents of this opinion have declared the concept of "group mind" to be mere metaphysics and that in reality the group is nothing other than the sum of the individuals.

To one who has watched the development of the concept of organism, whole, or Gestalt, in psychology this argumentation sounds strangely familiar. In the beginning of Gestalt theory, at the time of Ehrenfels, one attributed to a psychological whole, such as a melody, a so-called Gestalt quality—that is, an additional entity like a group mind, which the whole was supposed to have in addition to the sum of its parts. Today we know that we do not need to assume a mystical Gestalt quality, but that any dynamical whole has properties of its own. The whole might be symmetric in spite of its parts being asymmetric, a whole might be unstable in spite of its parts being stable in themselves.

As far as I can see, the discussion regarding group versus individual in sociology follows a similar trend. Groups are sociological wholes; the unity of these sociological wholes can be defined operationally in the same way as a unity of any other dynamic whole, namely, by the interdependence of its parts. Such a definition takes mysticism out of the group conception and brings the problem down to a thoroughly empirical and testable basis. At the same time it means a full recognition of the fact that properties of a social group, such as its organization, its stability, its goals, are something different from the organization, the stability, and the goals of the individuals in it.

How, then, should one describe a group? Let us discuss the effect of democratic, autocratic and laissez faire atmospheres or clubs which have been experimentally created by R. Lippitt, and by R. Lippitt and R. K. White, at the Iowa Child Welfare Research Station. Let us assume the club had five members and five observers were available. It might seem the simplest way always to assign one observer to one member of the club. However, the result at best would be five parallel micro-biographies of five individuals. This procedure would not yield a satisfactory record even of such simple facts of the group life as its organization, its sub-groups, and its leader-member relationship, not to speak of such important facts as the general atmosphere. Therefore, instead of assigning every observer to one individual, one observer was assigned to record from minute to minute the or-

ganization of the group into subgroups, another the social interactions, etc. In other words, instead of observing the properties
of individuals, the properties of the group as such were observed.

In one additional point sociology may well profit from psychology. It is a commonplace that the behavior of individuals as
well as groups depends upon their situation and their peculiar
position in it. In my mind the last decade of psychology has shown
that it is possible to give a clearly detailed description of the
peculiar structure of a concrete situation and its dynamics in
scientific terms. It can even be done in exact mathematical terms.
The youngest discipline of geometry called "topology" is an excellent tool with which to determine the pattern of the life-
space of an individual, and to determine within this life-space the
relative positions which the different regions of activity or persons, or groups of persons bear to each other. It has become possible
to transform into mathematical terms such everyday statements as:
"He is now closer to his goal of being a first-rate physician," "He
has changed the direction of his actions," or "He has joined a
group." In other words, it is possible to determine, in a geomet-
rically precise manner, the position, direction, and distance within
the life-space, even in such cases where the position of the person
and the direction of his actions are not physical but social in
nature. With this in mind let us return to the social experiment
which was undertaken at the Iowa Child Welfare Research Station.

II.

It is well known that the amount of success a teacher has in
the classroom depends not only on her *skill* but to a great extent
on the *atmosphere* she creates. This atmosphere is something in-
tangible; it is a property of the social situation as a whole, and
might be measured scientifically if approached from this angle.
As a beginning, therefore, Lippitt selected a comparison between
a democratic and an autocratic atmosphere for his study. The
purpose of his experiment was not to duplicate any given autocracy
or democracy or to study an "ideal" autocracy or democracy, but
to create set-ups which would give insight into the underlying

group dynamics. Two groups of boys and girls, ten and eleven years of age, were chosen for a mask-making club from a group of eager volunteers of two different school classes. With the help of the Moreno test both groups were equated as much as possible on such qualities as leadership and interpersonal relations. There were eleven meetings of the groups, the democratic group meeting always two days ahead of the autocratic one. The democratic group chose its activities freely. Whatever they chose the autocratic group was then ordered to do. In this way the activities of the group were equated. On the whole, then, everything was kept constant except the group atmosphere.

The leader in both groups was an adult student. He tried to create the different atmospheres by using the following technique:

Democratic	*Authoritarian*
1. All policies a matter of group determination, encouraged and drawn out by the leader.	1. All determination of policy by the strongest person (leader).
2. Activity perspective given by an explanation of the general steps of the process during discussion at first meeting (clay mould, plaster of Paris, papier-mâché, etc.). Where technical advice was needed, the leader tried to point out two or three alternative procedures from which choice could be made.	2. Techniques and steps of attaining the goal (completed mask) dictated by the authority, one at a time, so that future direction was always uncertain to a large degree.
3. The members were free to work with whomever they chose and the division of tasks was left up to the group.	3. The authority usually determined autocratically what each member should do and with whom he should work.
4. The leader attempted to be a group member in spirit and in discussion but not to perform	4. The dominator criticized and praised individual's activities *without giving objective rea-*

much of the actual work. He gave objective praise and criticism.

sons, and remained aloof from active group participation. He was always impersonal rather than outwardly hostile or friendly (a necessary concession in method).

During the meetings of the two groups, the observers noted the number of incidents and actions per unit of time. It was observed that the autocratic leader put forth about twice as much action towards the members as the democratic leader, namely, 8.4 actions as against 4.5. This difference is even greater if one takes into account only the initiated social approach, namely, 5.2 as against 2.1. Still greater is this difference in relation to ascendant or initiated ascendant behavior: the ascendant actions of the autocratic leader were nearly three times as frequent as those of the democratic leader.

In regard to submissive actions, the proportion was opposite, namely, more frequent by the democratic leader, although in both groups submissive actions of the leader were relatively rare. A similar relation held for the objective, matter-of-fact actions. Here too the democratic leader showed a higher frequency.

On the whole, then, there existed a much greater impact on the members of the group by the leader in autocracy than in democracy, and the approach was much more ascendant and less matter-of-fact.

When we attempt to answer the question "How does the leader compare with the ordinary member in an autocracy and a democracy?" we must refer to an ideal average member who is a statistical representation of what would happen if all activities were distributed equally among the members of the group, including the leader. In Lippitt's experiment the figures showed two facts clearly: first, in both groups the leader was really leading. The autocratic leader showed 118 per cent more initiated ascendant acts than the average ideal member, and the democratic leader 41 per cent more. Both leaders were less submissive than the average member, namely, the autocrat 78 per cent, the democrat

53 per cent. It was interesting to note that both showed also more matter-of-fact action than the average ideal member.

However, the difference between the ordinary member and the leader was much less pronounced in democracy than in autocracy, both in ascendant and submissive action. The democratic leader distinguished himself, also relatively, more by his greater matter-of-factness.

What do these figures indicate about the situation in which the autocratic and democratic group members find themselves? I can only mention a few aspects: In the autocratic group it is the leader who sets the policy. For instance, a child says: "I thought we decided to do the other mask." The leader answers: "No, *this* is the one *I* decided last time would be the best one." In dynamical terms such an incident means that the child would have been able to reach his own goal but the leader puts up a barrier against this locomotion. Instead he induces another goal for the child and a force in this direction. We are calling such goals, set up by the power of another person, an *induced* goal.

A parallel example in the democratic group might be this: A child asks, "How big will we make the mask? Are they out of clay or what?" The leader answers: "Would you like me to give you a little idea of how people generally make masks?" In other words, the leader in the democratic group, instead of hindering the children in getting to their own goal, bridges over whatever regions of difficulty might exist. For the democratic group, many paths are open; for the autocratic only one, namely, that determined by the leader. In an autocracy the leader determines not only the kind of activity but also who should work with whom. In our experimental democracy all work co-operation was the result of spontaneous sub-grouping of the children. In the autocracy 32 per cent of the work groups were initiated by the leader, as against 0 per cent in the democracy.

On the whole, then, the autocratic atmosphere gives a much greater and more aggressive dominance of the leader, and a narrowing down of the free movement of the members, together with a weakening of their power fields.

III.

What is the effect of this atmosphere on the group life of the children? As measured by the observers the child-to-child relationship was rather different in the two atmospheres. There was about thirty times as much hostile domination in the autocracy as in the democracy, more demands for attention and much more hostile criticism; whereas in the democratic atmosphere co-operation and praise of the other fellow was much more frequent. In the democracy more constructive suggestions were made and a matter-of-fact or submissive behavior of member to member was more frequent.

In interpreting these data, we might say that the "style of living and thinking" initiated by the leader dominated the relations between the children. In the autocracy instead of a co-operative attitude, a hostile and highly personal attitude became prevalent. This was strikingly brought out by the amount of group or "we" feeling as against "I" feeling: Statements which were "we-centered" occurred twice as often in the democracy as in the autocracy, whereas far more statements in the autocracy were "I-centered" than in the democracy.

So far as the relation of the children toward the leader was concerned, the statistical analysis revealed that the children in the autocratic group who were *less submissive* to each other were about *twice* as submissive to their leader, as the children in the democratic group. Initiated approaches to the leader in the democratic group were less frequent than in the autocratic group. In autocracy the action by the member toward the leader had more the character of a *response* to an approach of the leader. The approach to the leader in the autocracy was more submissive, or kept at least on a matter-of-fact basis.

On the whole, then, the style of living in both atmospheres governed the child-child relation as well as the child-leader relation. In the autocratic group the children were less matter-of-fact, less co-operative, and submissive toward their equals, but more submissive to their superior than in the democracy.

Behind this difference of behavior lie a number of factors. The tension is greater in the autocratic atmosphere, and the dynamic structure of both groups is rather different. In an autocratic group there are two clearly distinguished levels of social status: the leader is the only one having higher status, the others being on an equally low level. A strong barrier kept up by the leader prevents any one from increasing his status by acquiring leadership. In a democratic atmosphere the difference in social status is slight and there exists no barrier against acquiring leadership.

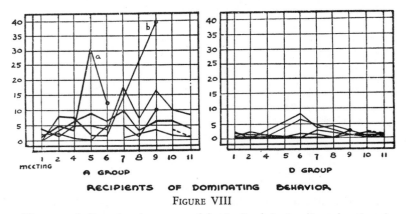

FIGURE VIII

The curves indicate that the amount of dominating behavior directed against the various individuals was much greater in autocracy (*A group*) than in democracy (*D group*). In autocracy two individuals (*a* and *b*) were treated as scapegoats (at the 5th and 6th, and at the 9th meetings respectively).

This has a rather clear effect on the amount of individuality. In our experiment every individual in the democracy showed a relatively greater individuality, having some field of his own in spite of the greater "we" feeling among them, or perhaps because of it. In the autocratic group on the contrary the children all had a low status without much individuality. The type of sub-grouping showed this difference even more clearly. In the autocracy, there was little "we" feeling and relatively little spontaneous sub-grouping among the children. If the work required the co-operation of four or five members, it was the leader who had to order the members to get together. In the democracy those groups came together spontaneously and they kept together about twice as long as in the autocracy. In the autocracy these larger units disintegrated much faster when left to themselves.

These group structures, in combination with the high tension in the autocracy, led in Lippitt's experiments to a *scapegoat* situation. The children in the autocratic group ganged together not against their leader, but against one of the children and treated him so badly that he ceased coming to the club. This happened to two different children during twelve sessions. Under autocratic rule any increase in status through leadership was blocked and the attempt to dominate was dictated by the style of living. In other words, every child became a potential enemy of every other one and the power fields of the children weakened each other, instead of strengthening each other by co-operation. Through combining in an attack against one individual the members who otherwise could not gain higher status were able to do so by violent suppression of one of their fellows.

One may ask whether these results are not due merely to individual differences. A number of facts rule out this explanation, although of course individual differences always play a role. Of particular interest was the transfer of one of the children from the autocratic to the democratic group, and of another from the democratic to the autocratic one. Before the transfer the difference between the two children was the same as between the two groups they belonged to, namely, the autocratic child was more dominating and less friendly and objective than the democratic one. However, after the transfer the behavior changed so that the previously autocratic child now became the less dominating and more friendly and objective child. In other words, the behavior of the children mirrored very quickly the atmosphere of the group in which they moved.

Later Lippitt and White studied four new clubs with other leaders. They included a third atmosphere, namely that of laissez faire, and exposed the same children successively to a number of atmospheres. On the whole, the results bear out those of Lippitt.

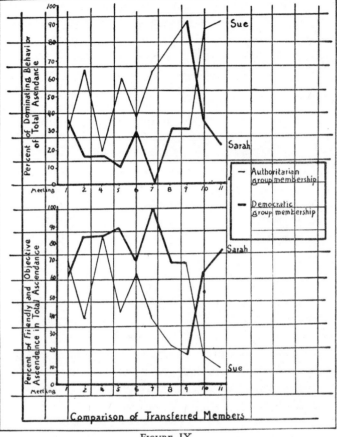

FIGURE IX

After the eighth meeting Sue was transferred from the democratic to the autocratic group, Sarah from the autocratic to the democratic group. The overt character of both children changed according to the atmosphere.

They show a striking difference between laissez faire and democ· racy very much in favor of democracy. They show further two types of reaction in the autocratic groups, one characterized by aggression, the second by apathy.

On the whole, I think there is ample proof that the difference in behavior in autocratic, democratic, and laissez faire situations is not a result of individual differences. There have been few experiences for me as impressive as seeing the expression in children's faces change during the first day of autocracy. The friendly, open, and co-operative group, full of life, became within a short half-hour a rather apathetic-looking gathering without initiative. The change from autocracy to democracy seemed to take somewhat more time than from democracy to autocracy. Autocracy is imposed upon the individual. Democracy he has to learn.

IV.

These experiments as a whole, then, bear out the observations of cultural anthropology and are well in line with other experiments on the effect of the situation as a whole. The social climate in which a child lives is for the child as important as the air it breathes. The group to which a child belongs is the ground on which he stands. His relation to this group and his status in it are the most important factors for his feeling of security or insecurity. No wonder that the group the person is a part of, and the culture in which he lives, determine to a very high degree his behavior and character. These social factors determine what space of free movement he has, and how far he can look ahead with some clarity into the future. In other words, they determine to a large degree his personal style of living and the direction and productivity of his planning.

It is a commonplace of today to blame the deplorable world situation on the discrepancy between the great ability of man to rule physical matter and his inability to handle social forces. This discrepancy in turn is said to be due to the fact that the development of the natural sciences has by far superseded the development of the social sciences.

No doubt this difference exists and it has been and is of great practical significance. Nevertheless, I feel this commonplace to be only half true, and it might be worth while to point to the other half of the story. Let us assume that it would be possible suddenly to raise the level of the social sciences to that of the natural sciences. Unfortunately this would hardly suffice to make the world a safe and friendly place to live in. Because the findings of the physical and the social sciences alike can be used by the gangster as well as by the physician, for war as well as for peace, for one political system as well as for another.

Internationally we still live essentially in a state of anarchy similar to that of the rule of the sword during medieval times. As long as no international agency exists which is able and willing to enforce international laws, national groups will always have to choose between bowing to international gangsterism and defending themselves.

It seems to be "natural" for people living in a thoroughly democratic tradition like that of the United States to believe that what is scientifically reasonable should finally become accepted everywhere. However, history shows, and experiments like the one I have described will, I think, prove anew, that the belief in reason as a social value is by no means universal, but is itself a result of a definite social atmosphere. To believe in reason means to believe in democracy, because it grants to the reasoning partners a status of equality. It is therefore not an accident that not until the rise of democracy at the time of the American and French Revolutions was the goddess of "reason" enthroned in modern society. And again, it is not accident that the first act of modern Fascism in every country has been officially and vigorously to dethrone this goddess and instead to make emotions and obedience the all-ruling principles in education and life from kindergarten to death.

I am persuaded that scientific sociology and social psychology based on an intimate combination of experiments and empirical theory can do as much, or more, for human betterment as the natural sciences have done. However, the development of such a realistic, nonmystical social science and the possibility of its fruitful application presuppose the existence of a society which believes in reason.

6

THE BACKGROUND OF
CONFLICT IN MARRIAGE

(1940)

THE GROUP AND THE INDIVIDUAL

A. *The social group as a fundamental determinant of the life space.*

MARRIAGE is a group situation, and, as such, shows the general characteristics of group life. The problems of a partner in marriage should therefore be viewed as arising from the relation between an individual and his group.

1. The group and its relation to other groups.

It is today widely recognized that a group is more than, or, more exactly, different from, the sum of its members. It has its own structure, its own goals, and its own relations to other groups. The essence of a group is not the similarity or dissimilarity of its members, but their interdependence. A group can be characterized as a "dynamical whole"; this means that a change in the state of any subpart changes the state of any other subpart. The degree of interdependence of the subparts of members of the group varies all the way from a loose "mass" to a compact unit. It depends, among other factors, upon the size, organization, and intimacy of the group.

a. A group might be a part of a more inclusive group. The married (*M*, Fig. Xa) are generally a part of a larger family, and the larger family (*Fa*) itself might be a part of a community (*C*) or of a nation.

b. The individual is usually a member of many more or less overlapping groups. He might be a member of a professional group (*Pr*, Fig. Xb), a political party (*Po*), a luncheon club (*L*), etc. The potency of any of these groups, that is, the degree to which a person's behavior is influenced by his membership in them, may be different for the different groups he belongs to.

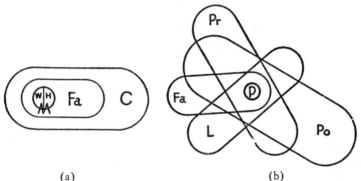

(a)

(b)

FIGURE Xa. THE MARRIAGE GROUP AS PART OF MORE INCLUSIVE GROUPS

    W, wife
    H, husband
    M, marriage group
    Fa, larger family
    C, community

FIGURE Xb. THE PERSON AS A MEMBER OF SEVERAL OVERLAPPING GROUPS

    P, person
    Fa, family
    Pr, professional group
    L, luncheon club
    Po, political party

For one person, business may be more important than politics; for another, the political party may have the higher potency. The potency of the different groups to which a person belongs varies with the momentary situation. When a person is at home the potency of the family is generally greater than when he is in his office. Marriage usually has a high potency within the world of an individual or, as one may say, his life-space.

2. What a group means to an individual.

a. The group as the ground on which a person stands. The speed and determination with which a person proceeds, his readiness to fight or to submit, and other important characteristics of his behavior depend upon the firmness of the ground on which he stands and upon his general security. The group a person belongs to is one of the most important constituents of this ground. If a person is not clear about his belongingness or if he is not well established within his group, his life-space will show the characteristics of an unstable ground.

b. The group as a means. Closely related to this is the fact that the group for the individual has often the position of a means. From early childhood the individual is accustomed to using a group relation, for instance, his relation to the mother, or to the family, as a means to achieving various physical and social goals. Later on, the prestige a person acquires because of belonging to a certain group, family, university, club, etc., is one of the important vehicles to his achievements: he is treated by the outsider as a part of this group.

c. The person as a part of a group. The change in the circumstances of an individual is to a great extent directly due to a change in the situation of the group of which he is a part. An attack upon his group, a rise or a decline of his group, means an attack upon him, a rise or a decline of his position. As a member of a group he, usually, has the ideals and goals one has in this group.

d. The group as a life-space. Finally the group is for the individual a part of the life-space in which he moves about. To reach or maintain a certain status or position within this group is one of the vital goals of the individual. His status in the group, the amount of space of free movement within it, and similar group properties, are important in determining the life-space of the individual. It will be clear at the outset how much marriage means in the life-space of the individual.

B. *The adaptation of the individual to the group.*

1. Group needs and individual freedom.

Belonging to a certain group does not mean that the individual must be in accord in every respect with the goals, regulations, and the style of living and thinking of the group. The individual has to a certain degree his own personal goals. He needs a sufficient space of free movement within the group to pursue those personal goals and to satisfy his individual wants. The problem of adaptation to, and successful living in, a group can be stated from the point of view of the individual in the following manner: How is it possible sufficiently to satisfy one's own individual needs without losing membership and status within the group? If the space of free movement of the individual within the group is too small, in other words, if his independence of the group is insufficient, the individual will be unhappy; too intense a frustration will force him to leave the group or will even destroy the group, if it limits the free movement of its members too severely.

2. Methods of adapting individual needs and group needs.

How the adjustment of the individual to the group has to be made depends upon the character of the group; the position of the individual within the group; the individual character of the person (especially the degree of independence he may need to be happy).

There are great differences in the manner in which individual and group needs are reconciled. The restrictions set up by the group may leave the individual much or little freedom. The restrictions may be based upon the democratic consent of the members of the group, or imposed by the will of an autocratic regime.

THE SPECIAL PROPERTIES OF THE MARRIAGE GROUP

The character of the marriage group within a given culture varies with nationality, race, occupation, and class. In addition there are, of course, very great variations in the structure of the individual marriage. Still, certain properties are characteristic for most marriage groups within our culture. In a consideration of conflicts in marriage, the following points seem to deserve special attention:

A. *The smallness of the group.*

The marriage group contains two adult members (husband, *H*, and wife, *W*, Fig. XIa), and perhaps one or more children (*C 1, 2, 3*, Fig. XIb). Because of the small number of members in the group, every move of one member will, relatively speaking, deeply affect the other members, and the state of the group. In other words, the smallness of the group makes its members very interdependent.

B. *The group touches central regions of the person.*

Marriage is very closely related to the vital problems and central layer of the person, to his values, fantasies, his social and economic status. Unlike other groups, marriage deals not merely with one or the other aspect of the person, but with his entire physical and social existence. Closely related to this point is the following.

C. *Intimate relation between members.*

Persons may have different "social distances" (willingness merely to live in the same town is characteristic of a greater social

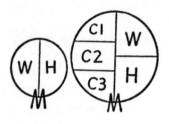

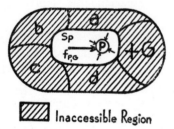

Inaccessible Region

(a)   (b)

FIGURE XI. THE MARRIAGE GROUP

M, marriage group
H, husband
C1, child
C2, child
C3, child

FIGURE XII. TENSION IN SITUATION OF FRUSTRATION AND NARROW SPACE OF FREE MOVEMENT

P, person   *G*, goal
Sp, space of free movement
a, b, c, d, inaccessible regions
$f_{P,G}$, force acting on *P* in the direction of *G*

distance than willingness to have dinner together). Willingness to marry is considered as a symptom of desire for the least social distance. Indeed, marriage means the willingness to share the activities and situations which otherwise are kept strictly private. Married life includes permanent physical proximity brought to a climax in the sex relationship. It involves closeness in situations of sickness, and sharing of other situations ordinarily hidden from third persons.

Every one of the points mentioned makes for a high degree of interdependence. Their combined effect produces one of the most closely integrated social units. That means, on the one hand, a high degree of so-called identification with the group and a readiness to stand together; on the other hand, great sensitivity to shortcomings of the partner or oneself.

CONFLICT IN MARRIAGE

A. *The general conditions of conflict.*

Experimental studies on individuals and groups show that one of the most important factors in the frequency of conflict and in the building up of an emotional outbreak is the general level of tension at which the person or group lives. Whether or not a particular event will lead to a conflict depends largely on the tension level or on the social atmosphere in the group. Among the causes for tension the following may be listed as outstanding:

1. The degree to which the needs of a person are in a state of hunger or satisfaction. A need in the state of hunger means not only that a particular region within the person is under tension but also that the person as a whole is on a higher tension level. This holds particularly for basic needs, such as sex or security.

2. The amount of space of free movement of the person. Too small a space of free movement generally leads to a high state of tension. This has been shown in experiments with anger and with democratic and autocratic group atmosphere. In an autocratic atmosphere the tension is much higher, resulting in apathy or aggression. (Fig. XII)

3. Outer barrier. Tension or conflict lead frequently to a tendency to leave the unpleasant situation. If this is possible, no high tension will develop. Lack of freedom to leave the situation as a result of either an "outer barrier" or an inner bond greatly favors the development of high tension and conflict.

4. Within the group life conflicts depend upon the degree to

which the goals of the members contradict each other, and upon the readiness to consider the other person's point of view.

B. *General considerations about conflicts in marriage.*

We have mentioned that the question of the adaptation of an individual to a group can be formulated in this way: How can an individual find enough space of free movement to satisfy his own personal needs within a group without interfering with the interests of the group? From the specific properties of the marriage group it follows that the securing of an adequate private sphere within this group is especially difficult. The group is small; it is intimate; the very essence of marriage involves sharing these private spheres with the other member of the group; the central

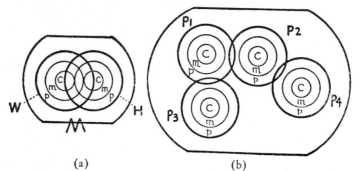

(a)   (b)

FIGURE XIII. DIFFERENT DEGREES OF INTIMACY BETWEEN GROUP MEMBERS

(a) Intimate relationship   (b) Superficial relationship

M, marriage group   *c*, central layer of the person
H, husband   *m*, medium layer of the person
W, wife   *p*, peripheral layer of the person
P1, P2, P3, P4, persons superficially
related

layers of the person and his very social existence are involved. Each member is particularly sensitive to everything not in accord with his own needs. If one represents the sharing of situations by an overlapping of these layers, marriage (*M*) might be represented by Fig. XIIIa, whereas a group with less intimate relation would correspond to Fig. XIIIb. It can be seen that it is easier for a member of group XIIIb to find freedom for satisfying his private needs without giving up the relatively superficial relations to the other members, than for a member of the group in Fig. XIIIa. This latter group situation is, therefore, likely to lead to certain conflicts. In marriage, as in any intimate group, these conflicts may become particularly deep and emotional.

C. *The need situation.*

1. The variety and contradictory nature of needs to be satisfied in marriage.

Manifold needs are generally expected to be satisfied in and through marriage. The husband may expect his wife to be, at the same time, sweetheart, comrade, housewife, mother, manager of his income or co-supporter of the family, and family representative in the social life of the community. The wife may expect her husband to be her sweetheart, comrade, supporter of the family, father, and caretaker of the house. These various functions which the partner in marriage is called upon to satisfy frequently demand opposite types of actions and personality traits. They are, therefore, not easily reconciled with each other. Nevertheless, failure to fulfill one of these functions may leave important needs unsatisfied, and result in a high and permanent level of tension in the group life.

Which of these needs are dominant, which are fully satisfied, which are partly satisfied, and which are not at all satisfied, depend upon the personality of the marriage partners, and upon the setting in which the particular marriage group lives. There is obviously an unlimited variety of patterns corresponding to the different degrees of satisfaction and importance of the various needs. The manner in which a partner reacts to these different constellations of satisfaction and frustration—with emotionality, a matter-of-fact attitude, struggle, or acceptance, realism—adds further to the variety of backgrounds one has to consider for an understanding of the conflicts within a particular marriage.

There are two more points inherent in the nature of needs, which might be mentioned in connection with conflicts in marriage.

Needs create tension not only in the state of hunger but also in the
state of oversatiation. Excess of consummatory actions leads to
oversatiation not only in the realm of bodily needs, such as sex,
but also of psychological needs, such as bridge-playing, cooking,
social activities, taking care of children, etc. The tension resulting
from oversatiation is in no way less intense or emotional than a
tension due to hunger. Therefore, if the amount of consummatory
action necessary for reaching the state of satisfaction is different
for the partners in marriage, a solution cannot always be found
by making the consummatory requirements of the more hungry
member the measure for the group life: this may well mean oversatiation for the less hungry partner. In regard to some needs,
like dancing or other social activities, the less easily satisfied
partner might look for satisfaction outside. But often, particularly
in regard to sexual needs, this cannot be done without resulting
in serious damage to married life.

We mentioned that conflicts are likely to be more serious when
central needs are involved. Unfortunately, there seems to be a
tendency for any need to become more central when in a state
of hunger or oversatiation, and more peripheral, that is less
important, when in the state of satisfaction. In other words, the
unsatisfied needs tend to dominate the situation. This obviously
increases the chances for conflicts.

2. The sexual need.

For marriage these general characteristics of needs are particularly important in their application to sexual needs. It has
often been stated that sex relations are bipolar, that they mean at
the same time devotion to and possession of another person.
Sexual desire and disgust are closely related, and one may quickly
turn into the other with the change of sexual hunger to satiation
or oversatiation. Neither the sexual rhythm nor the particular
manner of sex satisfaction can be expected to be identical in both
persons. Besides, there is often a periodical increase of nervous-
ness in the woman, related to the menstrual period.

All of these factors may lead to more or less difficult conflicts,
and they imply the necessity of mutual adaptation. If within this

realm no balance can be found which will give sufficient satisfaction to both partners, it will be difficult to keep the marriage intact.

If the discrepancies between the partners are not too wide, and the marriage has a sufficient positive value for the persons involved, a balance will probably be found in the long run. A most important factor affecting both happiness and conflict in marriage is, therefore, the position and the meaning marriage has within the life-space of husband and wife.

3. Security.

I may mention specifically but one additional want (although it seems doubtful to me whether one can classify it as a "need"), that is, the need for security. We pointed out that one of the outstanding general properties of a social group is its character as the ground on which the individual stands. If this ground is unstable, the individual will feel insecure and become tense. Persons are generally very sensitive even to the slightest increases in the instability of their social ground.

The role which the marriage group plays as a social ground for the individual is certainly of prime importance. The marriage group constitutes a "social home" where the person feels accepted, sheltered, and reassured of his worth. This may be the reason why women list lack of truthfulness and of economic success on the part of the husband among the most frequent causes for unhappiness in marriage. Indeed, even unfaithfulness may not reduce the intellectual clarity about one's own situation and affect the stability of a common social ground as much as distrust does. Distrust of the partner in marriage makes one uncertain of where one stands and in what direction an intended action actually points.

D. *The space of free movement.*

A sufficient space of free movement within a group is a condition for fulfillment of the individual's needs and for the adaptation to the group. An insufficient space of free movement leads, as we mentioned, to tension.

1. Close interdependence and space of free movement.

The marriage group includes relatively few persons; it means sharing house, table, and bed; and touches very deep layers of the person. Every one of these facts implies that practically every action of one member impinges to some extent on the other. This naturally means a decisive narrowing of the individual's space of free movement.

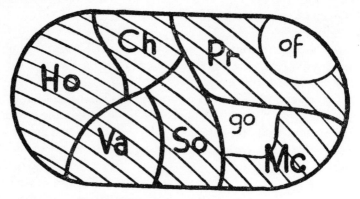

FIGURE XIV. LIFE-SPACE OF HUSBAND

The shaded areas indicate the regions more or less influenced by the wife. The husband's space of free movement (white areas) is narrowed by the loving interest of the wife.

Pr. professional life	*Va,* vacation	*of,* office life
Mc, men's club	*Ch,* children	*go,* playing golf
Ho, home management	*So,* social life	

2. Love and space of free movement

Love has a natural tendency to be all-inclusive, to embrace the whole life of the other person, his past, present, and future. It tends to sway all his activities, his business affairs, his relation with other persons, etc. Fig. XIV represents the effect which the love of the wife may have on the life-space of the husband outside the marriage.

It is clear that the tendency of love to be all-embracing directly endangers the basic condition for the adjustment of a person to a group, namely, a sufficient space of privacy. Even if the spouse enters these regions of activities with a sympathetic attitude he deprives the partner of some of his freedom.

In some respects the marriage situation makes the problems resulting from love even more difficult. Ordinarily membership in a group implies the sharing of only certain types of situations and requires mutual acceptance only with regard to particular properties of the person. For instance, when one joins a business association, honesty and certain abilities are usually sufficient qualifications. Even in a circle of friends it is generally possible to arrange the situation so that they can enjoy the properties liked in each other, but avoid those situations which they don't like to share. The story of two families which are friendly and see much of each other until they decide to spend the summer vacation in the same house, when they promptly cease to be friends, is a typical example of how a setting which takes away privacy might spoil friendship. Marriage involves the necessity of saying "yes" to both the agreeable and disagreeable qualities of the partners and the willingness to live permanently in close contact.

How much privacy is necessary depends on the character of the individual concerned. It depends also on the meaning marriage has in the life-spaces of both individuals.

E. *The meaning of marriage in the life-space of an individual.*

1. Marriage as help or hindrance.

Let us compare the situation of a bachelor and a married man. The life-space of the bachelor is dominated by certain major goals (G, Fig. XVa). He is trying to overcome the difficulties (B) which lie between him and his goals.

After marriage, many of these goals will still be the same, and again some barriers will have to be overcome if he wishes to reach his objectives. But now, as a member of a family (M, Fig. XVb), responsible, for instance, for its livelihood, he will have to overcome these barriers no longer as a single person, but "carrying the burden of a family." That may involve greater difficulties. If these become too great, marriage itself might acquire a negative valence; it will assume the character of an obstacle in his path. On the other hand, marriage might be helpful in overcoming barriers. That does not refer only to financial assistance by his wife. It applies to all kinds of social achievements. It might be mentioned that today children are economically more of a burden and less of a help than previously, although, for the farmer, children are still on the whole an asset.

2. Home life and outside activities.

Differences in the meaning of marriage for both partners may express themselves in the different answers given to the question

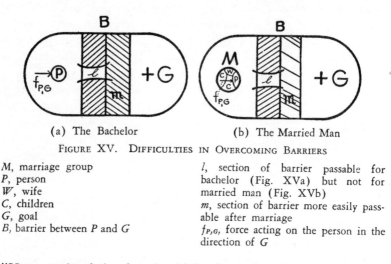

(a) The Bachelor　　　　　　　　(b) The Married Man

FIGURE XV.　DIFFICULTIES IN OVERCOMING BARRIERS

M, marriage group	l, section of barrier passable for bachelor (Fig. XVa) but not for married man (Fig. XVb)
P, person	
W, wife	
C, children	m, section of barrier more easily passable after marriage
G, goal	
B, barrier between P and G	$f_{P,G}$, force acting on the person in the direction of G

"How much of the day should be devoted to home life?" Frequently, the husband tends to give more time to activities outside the home than the wife, whose main interest may lie in housework and children. Women often have more profound interests in personality and personality development than men, who tend to think more of so-called "objective achievements."

This situation is represented in Fig. XVI. The actual time devoted to family life expresses a balance of forces resulting from the interests of husband and wife. If the discrepancy between the needs of the partners is too wide, a more or less permanent conflict is likely to ensue. Similar discrepancies may arise regarding the time to be allowed for particular activities, such as recreation and society life.

3. Harmony and discrepancy in the meaning of marriage.

Conflicts generally do not become really serious so long as the meaning of marriage in the life-spaces of both partners is not too divergent.

The meaning marriage has for an individual varies greatly. Often marriage means something more important or more inclu-

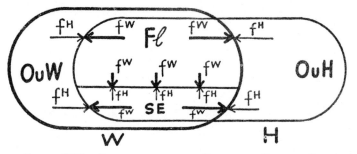

FIGURE XVI. CONFLICT AS TO THE EXTENT OF COMMON LIFE

In the situation represented here, the husband wishes to decrease, the wife to increase, the extent of family life; in regard to sex life, the opposite is true.

W, wife's activities
H, husband's activities
Fl, common family life
OuW, activities of wife outside common life

OuH, activities of husband outside common life
SE, sex life
F^W, force corresponding to wife's wishes
F^H, force corresponding to husband's wishes

sive for the wife than for the husband. In our society the professional field is ordinarily more important for the husband than it is for the wife, and hence, for him, the relative weight of any other field is decreased.

Marriage may mean for both husband and wife something relatively arbitrary, a means to an end, such as social influence and power. Or it may be an end in itself including the rearing of children, or simply living together. Rearing of children, too, may mean very different things for different individuals.

It is usual for marriage to mean different things for each of the partners. This in itself does not necessarily lead to conflict. If the wife is more interested in the rearing of children she will want to spend more time at home. That need not interfere with the interest of the husband and may even lead to greater harmony. A discrepancy of interests gives rise to difficulties only if the different meanings husband and wife attach to their marriage cannot be realized simultaneously.

F. *Overlapping groups.*

In modern society every individual is a member of a variety of groups. Husband and wife usually belong partly to different groups. These groups may have conflicting goals and ideologies. Not infrequently, conflict in marriage results from loyalties to these overlapping groups, and the general atmosphere of a marriage is to a large extent determined by the character of these groups.

Obviously, this question plays an important role in case husband and wife belong to different racial or religious groups or to widely divergent social or economic classes. Much of what we discussed under the heading of needs and the meaning of marriage might be dealt with here, for many of a person's needs are directly related to his membership in certain groups, such as business groups, political parties, etc.

We will mention here specifically only two examples.

1. Marriage and the larger family.

The newly established marriage sometimes has to face difficulties resulting from the ties of the partners to the families from which they come. The wife's mother may consider her son-in-law just an addition to her family; or each of the in-law families involved may try to draw the new unit to its side. This may lead to conflict, especially if the relation between the two families is not friendly to begin with.

The possibility of conflict between husband and wife is minimized if the potency of their membership in the marriage group is higher than that of their respective memberships in the older groups. For, in this case, the marriage group will act as a unit in regard to the conflict. If however, the ties to the older families are still strong (Fig. XVII) husband and wife will actually be dominated by their membership in different groups and a conflict is likely to arise. This probably lies behind the often-heard advice to a new couple "not to stand too close to their families."

2. Jealousy.

Jealousy is most common; it can be found already in young children; it can be most vivid even when it is contrary to all reason. Emotional jealousy is based partly on the feeling that one's "prop-

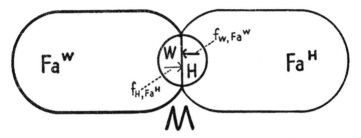

FIGURE XVII. THE MARRIAGE GROUP AS A UNIT AND AS PART OF THE LARGER FAMILY

H, husband
W, wife
Fa^H, family of husband
Fa^W, family of wife
M, marriage group

f_H, Fa^H, force acting on husband in direction of his family
f_W, Fa^W, force acting on wife in direction of her family

erty" is taken away. It is understandable, from the great amount of overlapping (represented in Fig. XIIIa), and from the tendency of love to be all-inclusive, that this feeling may be easily aroused if the relation between two persons is very close.

The intimate relation of one partner to a third person not only makes the second partner "lose" the first one, but the second partner will have, in addition, the feeling that something of his own intimate life is thrown open to a third person. By permitting his marriage partner to enter his intimate life, he did not mean to throw it open to the public. The relation of the partner to the third person is felt as a breach in the barrier between one's intimate life and the public.

It is important to understand why situations of this kind might be experienced differently by each partner. The life-space of the husband might be represented through Fig. XVIIIa. His friendship to the third person (fr) might have grown out of his business relations. It may have become a rather important region for him personally, while still retaining its place in the business region, or at least clearly outside his marriage (M) life. For the husband, therefore, there is no interference between his married life and his relation to the third person: Nothing is taken away

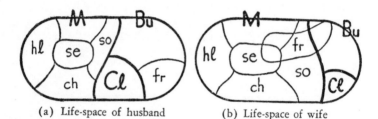

(a) Life-space of husband   (b) Life-space of wife

FIGURE XVIII. DIFFERENT MEANINGS OF THE SAME EVENT IN THE LIFE-SPACES OF HUSBAND AND WIFE

In the life-space of the husband the region "friendship of husband with third person" does not overlap with the "marriage region"; it definitely overlaps in the life-space of the wife.

M, marriage region
Bu, business life of husband
Cl, club life of husband
hl, home life
ch, life with children

se, sexual relation between husband and wife
so, social life of husband and wife
fr, friendship of husband with third person

from marriage (M), and the two loyalties are hardly conflicting. The same situation may appear in an entirely different light to the wife. In her life-space (Fig. XVIIIb), the whole life of the husband is embraced in the marriage relation and particularly any kind of friendly or intimate relation profoundly affects the marriage region. To the wife, therefore, this appears as a definite invasion of the marriage sphere.

G. *Marriage as a group in the making.*

The sensitivity of the group to the move of each member is especially great in the early period of marriage. Like a young organism, a young group is more flexible. As husband and wife come to know each other, a way of handling their marriage prob- lems gets established. To alter this established way may become difficult after a time. To some extent society provides a traditional form which gives shape to the new marriage. But recent emphasis on the private character of marriage makes the atmosphere of the group dependent to even a higher degree upon the character and responsibility of the partners.

In the young marriage the situation is not clear in regard to the balance between one's own needs and those of the partner. That leads to typical conflicts, but at the same time allows greater flexibility for their solution.

SOLUTION OF CONFLICTS

Whether a conflict may be solved, to what degree, and in what way, depends entirely upon the constellation of the particular mar- riage, and the meaning of the conflict for it. I should like, how- ever, to point to one factor specifically: We have mentioned that the frequency and seriousness of conflicts in marriage depend mainly on the general atmosphere of the marriage. For the solution of conflicts the atmosphere again seems to be the most important factor.

Being married presupposes the relinquishing of a certain amount of freedom. This may be done in two ways: one may sacrifice one's freedom for the sake of marriage, and resign oneself to frustra- tion; or one may make the marriage so much a part of one's own life that the goals of the partner become to a high degree one's own goals. It is clear that in the latter case, it is not quite correct to speak of a sacrifice: the meaning of the "limitation of one's freedom" is now considerably different.

There is no mystical power behind such "identification" with the other partner, and it is not a special characteristic of love and marriage. Relinquishing of a certain amount of freedom is a condition of membership in any group. It is therefore important for every group to know on what basis the balance between individual and group needs is established. Compliance with the rules of the group may be more or less enforced, or may result from a strong "we-feeling." Experiments show that the latter is much more characteristic of certain democratic atmospheres than of certain autocratic atmospheres. They further show that "we-feeling" makes for less tension and conflict. The readiness to consider the other member's views and goals and to discuss personal problems rationally leads to quicker solution of conflicts. Doubtless the same holds for the atmosphere in marriage:

> I was angry with my friend:
> I told my wrath, my wrath did end.
> I was angry with my foe:
> I told it not, my wrath did grow.

7

TIME PERSPECTIVE AND MORALE

(1942)

STUDIES in unemployment show how a long-drawn-out idleness affects all parts of a person's life. Thrown out of a job, the individual tries to keep hoping. When he finally gives up, he frequently restricts his action much more than he has to. Even though he has plenty of time, he begins to neglect his home duties. He may cease to leave his immediate neighborhood; even his thinking and his wishes become narrow. This atmosphere spreads to the children, and they, too, become narrow-minded even in their ambitions and dreams. In other words, the individual and the family as a whole present a complete picture of low morale.

An analysis of this behavior shows the importance of that psychological factor which commonly is called "hope." Only when the person gives up hope does he stop "actively reaching out"; he loses his energy, he ceases planning, and, finally, he even stops wishing for a better future. Only then does he shrink to a primitive and passive life.

Hope means that "sometime in the future, the real situation will be changed so that it will equal my wishes." Hope means a similarity between the individual's "level of expectation" and his "irreality level of wishes." The picture presented by this "psychological future" seldom corresponds to what actually happens later. The individual may see his future as too rosy or too bleak; frequently the character of the psychological future vacillates between hope and despair. But, regardless of whether the individual's picture of the future is correct or incorrect at a given time, this picture deeply affects the mood and the action of the individual at that time.

The psychological future is part of what L. K. Frank has called "time perspective." The life-space of an individual, far from being limited to what he considers the present situation, includes the future, the present, and also the past. Actions, emotions, and certainly the morale of an individual at any instant depend upon his total time perspective.

The conduct of the unemployed, then, is an example of how time perspective may lower morale. How morale may, on the contrary, be heightened by time perspective is illustrated by the conduct of the Zionists in Germany shortly after Hitler came to power. The great majority of Jews in Germany had believed for decades that the pogroms of Czarist Russia "couldn't happen here." When Hitler came to power, therefore, the social ground on which they stood suddenly was swept from under their feet. Naturally, many became desperate and committed suicide; with nothing to stand on, they could see no future life worth living.

The time perspective of the numerically small Zionist group, on the other hand, had been different. Although they too had not considered pogroms in Germany a probability, they had been aware of their possibility. For decades they had tried to study their own sociological problems realistically, advocating and promoting a program that looked far ahead. In other words, they had a time perspective which included a psychological past of surviving adverse conditions for thousands of years and a meaningful and inspiring goal for the future. As the result of such a time perspective, this group showed high morale—despite a present which was judged by them to be no less foreboding than by others. Instead of inactivity and encystment in the face of a difficult situation—a result of such limited time perspective as that characteristic of the unemployed—the Zionists with a long-range and realistic time perspective showed initiative and organized planning. It is worth noticing how much the high morale of this small group contributed to sustaining the morale of a large section of the non-Zionist Jews of Germany. Here, as in many other cases, a small group with high morale became a rallying point for larger masses.

Time perspective seems, indeed, to be sufficiently important for morale to warrant a more thorough analysis.

DEVELOPMENT OF TIME PERSPECTIVE

The infant lives essentially in the present. His goals are immediate goals; when he is distracted, he "forgets" quickly. As an individual grows older, more and more of his past and his future affect his present mood and action. The goals of the school child may already include promotion to the next grade at the end of the year. Years later, as the father of a family, the same person will often think in terms of decades when planning his life. Practically everyone of consequence in the history of humanity—in religion, politics, or science—has been dominated by a time perspective which has reached out far into future generations, and which frequently was based on an awareness of an equally long past. But a large time perspective is not peculiar to great men. A hundred and thirty billion dollars of life insurance in force in the United States offer an impressive bit of evidence for the degree to which a relatively distant psychological future, not connected with the well-being of one's own person, affects the everyday life of the average citizen.

Aside from the broadness of the time perspective, there is a further aspect important for morale. The young child does not distinguish clearly between fantasy and reality. To a great extent wishes and fears affect his judgment. As an individual becomes mature and gains "self-control," he more clearly separates his wishes from his expectations: his life space differentiates into a "level of reality" and various "levels of irreality," such as fantasy and dream.

TENACITY AND TIME PERSPECTIVE

"Tenacity in the face of adversity is the most unequivocal index of high morale." This is an idea widely accepted as the essence of military morale. While there may be some question as to whether the ability to persist in the face of difficulties is actually the most fundamental aspect of morale, unquestionably it is one aspect of either civilian or military morale, and as such is a good starting point for discussion.

If morale means the ability to "take it," to face disagreeable or dangerous situations, one must ask first, "What constitute disagreeable or dangerous situations for an individual?" Ordinarily, we are accustomed to think of physical pain or bodily danger; yet anyone who climbs mountains or explores jungles for pleasure, any boy who drives an automobile fast, or who plays football shows that this answer is too simple.

(*a*) *The disagreeable and time perspective.* Under ordinary circumstances, an individual will strongly resist an order to pick up mercury from the floor with a wooden spoon, or to eat three dozen unsalted soda crackers. As "subjects" in an experiment, on the other hand, individuals were found ready to "take it" without either hesitation or resistance. In other words, whether or not an activity is disgraceful or unpleasant depends to a high degree on its psychological "meaning," that is, on the larger unit of events of which this action forms a part. In the role of a patient, for example, the individual permits as "treatment" by the doctor what would otherwise be vigorously resisted because of bodily pain or social unpleasantness.

A good example of the degree to which the meaning of the larger psychological units and the time perspective affect the felt pain and the morale of the individual is provided by M. L. Farber's study of suffering in prison. It was found that the prison work which the individual has to do day by day has no appreciable correlation with the amount of his suffering. Individuals who suffered much were quite as likely to hold advantageous jobs so far as power and leisure were concerned (such as editor of the prison magazine or runner for the deputy warden) as to hold the most disadvantageous or unpaid of prison jobs. (The correlation between the amount of suffering and the "objective" advantage of the prison job was .01.) There was little negative correlation between the subjective satisfaction which the prisoner felt in his prison job and the amount of his suffering $(r = -.19)$. A definite relation, on the other hand, did exist between the amount of suffering and certain factors connected with the future or past—a man's feeling, for instance, that his sentence was unjust $(r = .57)$, or his hope of "getting a break" in regard to release $(r = -.39)$. This relation held true, moreover, in spite of the fact that the release might be expected to take place only after a number of years. The *actual* length of the sentence and the length of the time served do not correlate strongly with the amount of suffering; however, a marked relationship does exist between the suffering and a man's *feeling* that he has served longer than he justly should have served $(r = .66)$.

Not present hardships in the usual sense of the term, then, but rather certain aspects of the psychological future and the psychological past, together with feelings of being treated fairly or unfairly, are most important in determining the amount of one's suffering. A factor of considerable weight for the amount of suffering in this case was uncertainty in regard to when parole might be granted $(r = .51)$. This factor, too, was one not related to the present immediate situation of the individual but was an aspect of his time perspective.

In solitary confinement, too, it has been frequently reported, one of the most painful experiences is the uncertainty as to how much time has elapsed. Once again, it is not a present hardship but certain characteristics of the time perspective which lend the situation its anguish.

(*b*) *Persistency and Time Perspective.* Even more than suffering, persistency depends on the time perspective of the individual. As long as there is hope that difficulties may be overcome for that price in effort and pain which the individual is ready to pay, he goes on trying. If the objective is worthy, indeed, the effort is not even felt to be a "sacrifice." Persistency, then, depends on two factors: the value of the goal and the outlook for the future. This holds both for child and adult, for soldier and civilian.

A few facts pertinent to morale, drawn from experiments with children, might be mentioned here. How soon the individual will give up in face of an obstacle depends, according to these experiments, on three factors: (1) the strength of the psychological force toward the goal (the persistency will be greater if the goal is more highly cherished or if the psychological distance to the goal is smaller); (2) the felt probability of reaching the goal (which, in turn, depends on past successes and failures and on the intellectual capacity of the individual); and (3) the degree of initiative of the individual.

The first point is identical with the felt value of the cause for which the effort is made. The second refers to the psychological future. The means whereby one can influence the psychological future so that a man's outlook will be optimistic is a point much discussed in regard to military morale. Everywhere the effect of the past on the future is emphasized; whereas nothing is more difficult than to keep up morale after a defeat, persistency is greatly strengthened by past victories. Nor need this past necessarily be one's own past. When the individual joins a "Fighting 69th," the tradition and history of this regiment become a part of his life-space. And only after he has demonstrated this fact will he be recognized as a true member.

Experimental data show that although past successes are most effective if they have been won in the same field of activity, nevertheless "substitute successes" and, to a lesser degree, mere praise and encouragement still bolster persistency. An individual may likewise be taught to be more persistent and to react less emotionally to obstacles if encouraging past experiences are built up. Persistency, indeed, is closely related to the social position of the individual, to his feeling of strength and security.

Passive individuals are on the average less persistent than active individuals; there are, however, certain exceptions. Individuals with low initiative sometimes show a kind of passive perseverance; they remain vis-à-vis the obstacle and keep up a gesturelike activity toward the goal. And some active individuals, on the other hand, quit very soon. Instead of waiting to be driven away slowly by an increasing number of failures, these individuals have sufficient initiative to make their decision as soon as realistic considerations indicate that the goal cannot be reached. The ability to make just such active decisions is recognized as one of the basic requirements for military leaders. A weak individual's gesturelike perseverance deprives him of the flexibility necessary for arriving at new, more efficient solutions. The readiness to make "realistic decisions" may sometimes, of course, be merely a front for a lack of willingness to see things through. We shall come back to this question later.

GROUP MORALE

Group morale depends on time perspective as much as does individual morale. Clearly demonstrative of this fact are French's controlled experiments with groups of individuals of college age who were placed in a physically disagreeable situation. The subjects were set to work in a room which slowly filled with smoke oozing in from under the door; and they knew that the doors were locked. After a while, the smoke became rather disagreeable. The reactions of the group varied from panic to laughter, depending mainly upon whether the smoke was construed as arising from an actual fire or as a hoax of the psychologist. The difference between these interpretations lies mainly in a difference in time perspective and in the felt degree of reality of the danger. The recent history of morale in France, England, and the United States is a vivid example of how much the degree to which the reality of a danger is acknowledged determines group goals and group action.[1]

A comparative study made of previously organized and non-organized groups in a situation of fear and of frustration showed the organized groups to be both more highly motivated and more persistent. They were less likely to disintegrate, although as a result of this stronger motivation they felt more highly frustrated in regard to group goals which could not be reached. Contrary to usual expectation, however, fear spread more quickly through the organized than the unorganized group, because of the higher interdependence among the members of the former. In a highly specific way these experiments verify our everyday experience that the

[1] See the postscript to this chapter.

morale of an individual faced with danger is highly dependent on the atmosphere of his group.

INITIATIVE, PRODUCTIVITY, GOAL LEVEL, AND TIME PERSPECTIVE

In Nazi Germany, morale is considered to be "a driving force which propels every unit of the political and military organization to exert maximum effort and capacity"; it "implies a positive state of mind of the individual and the mass toward a uniform goal." Such a concept of morale mirrors the training necessary for an offensive war and totalitarian uniformity. Experimental psychology indicates, however, that one element in this concept is correct for every type of morale. Tenacity in the face of obstacles, the ability to "take it on the chin," is merely one aspect of a more fundamental state of the person which may be characterized as a combination of initiative and a determination to reach certain goals, to realize certain values.

Given comparable settings, the morale of an individual or a group might be measured by the quality and quantity of its achievement, that is, by its productivity. Initiative and productivity, dependent as they are on the proper balance of a variety of factors, are highly sensitive to changes in this balance. Here physical well-being plays a significant role. Today, every country is aware of the importance of sufficient food and vitamins for civilian morale. An oversatiated individual, on the other hand, is by no means likely to show the greatest initiative and productivity. Subtle psychological factors play a great role in morale, and Hitler's plans of offensive warfare rightly consider the civilian morale of the enemy country as one of its most vulnerable and important points for attack.

PRODUCTIVITY AND A TIME PERSPECTIVE OF INSECURITY AND UNCERTAINTY

Experiments with children help us isolate some of the psychological factors determining initiative and productivity. For the situations of childhood are easily controlled by the all-powerful adult, and children probably show more quickly than adults those basic reactions on which the psychology of large masses depends

If the free play activity of a child is interfered with, his average level of productivity may regress, for instance, from the age level of five and a half years to the much lower level of productivity of the three-and-a-half-year-old child. This regression is closely related to the child's time perspective. Because the adult has stopped the child in the midst of play of great interest and productivity, now he feels himself to be on insecure ground; he is aware of the possibility that the overwhelming power of the adult may interfere again at any moment. This "background of insecurity and frustration" not only has a paralyzing effect on long-range planning; it also lowers initiative and the level of productivity.

The effect of interference is particularly severe if the individual is left in the dark as to the character of the new situation. The negative, nonspecific command, "Don't!" lowers initiative and productivity considerably more than a command to change to a different but specific task. Indeed, one of the main techniques for breaking morale through a "strategy of terror" consists in exactly this tactic—keep the person hazy as to where he stands and just what he may expect. If in addition frequent vacillations between severe disciplinary measures and promises of good treatment, together with the spreading of contradictory news, make the "cognitive structure" of the situation utterly unclear, then the individual may cease to know even whether a particular plan would lead toward or away from his goal. Under these conditions, even those individuals who have definite goals and are ready to take risks will be paralyzed by severe inner conflicts in regard to what to do.

Pairs of strong friends, it is interesting to note, regress less in a background of frustration than do pairs of children who are not friends. Their greater tolerance for frustration seems to be due to a feeling of greater security among friends, as indicated, for instance, by a greater readiness to attack the experimenter as the source of frustration. Here is an example of how group "belongingness" may increase a feeling of security, thereby raising the morale and the productivity of an individual.

The initiative of a child and his productivity have been found, moreover, to be greater in the co-operative play of pairs of children than in solitary play—both in situations of frustration and in situations of nonfrustration. The increased productivity of an individual as a member of a group as compared with his productivity as a lone individual is a factor of prime importance for civilian morale. Bearing out this point, a study of factory workers indicates that, aside from security, personal attention given to the individual plays a role in raising the level of productivity, probably because of the resultant increase in his feeling of "belongingness."

This finding is but one of many which pertain to age differences, individual differences, the effect of different situations, and the difference between the activity of individuals and groups—all of which indicate that productivity depends upon the number of diversified abilities and needs that can be integrated into an organized, unified endeavor. It is the principle of "diversity within unity" which dominates productivity, the principle that is so basic to a democratic solution of the problem of minorities and to democratic living in all types of groups, from small face-to-face groups to world organization.

In some cases, paradoxically, a certain amount of frustration or difficulty actually increases productivity; such seems to be the case if the individual previously has not been fully involved and if the difficulty serves as a fuse to touch off an all-out effort. Closely related to this result is one of the most fundamental problems of morale, namely: where will the individual or the group set its goal? What will be its level of aspiration?

LEVEL OF ASPIRATION AND TIME PERSPECTIVE

The three-month-old infant is as happy when someone hands him a toy as when he gets it by his own efforts. But the child of two or three years frequently rejects the help of another person, preferring to get by his own action an object that is difficult to reach. He prefers, in other words, a difficult path and a difficult goal to an easy path and an easy goal. This behavior of human beings, seemingly paradoxical, is certainly contrary to a belief which is widely accepted and which deeply influences thinking.

even about politics—the belief that human beings are led by the "pleasure principle" along the easiest road to the easiest goal. Actually, from childhood on, the goals which an individual sets in his daily life and for his long-range plans are influenced by his ideology, by the group to which he belongs, and by a tendency to raise his level of aspiration to the upper limit of his ability.

On this problem experiments have yielded considerable knowledge—how the level of aspiration develops during childhood, how success and failure in one field affect the level of aspiration in other fields, how the individual reacts to "too difficult" or "too easy" tasks, and how the standards of groups influence his own goal level.

The setting up of goals is closely related to time perspective. The goal of the individual includes his expectations for the future, his wishes, and his daydreams. Where the individual places his goals will be determined fundamentally by two factors, namely, by the individual's relations to certain values and by his sense of realism in regard to the probability of reaching the goal. The frames of reference which determine the values of success and failure vary considerably from individual to individual and from group to group. By and large, there is a tendency in our society to raise the level of aspiration toward the limit of the individual's ability. The principle of realism, on the other hand, tends to safeguard the individual against failure and to keep ambition down to earth. How high the individual can set his goal and still keep in touch with the reality level is one of the most important factors for his productivity and his morale.

A successful individual typically sets his next goal somewhat, but not too much, above his last achievement. In this way he steadily raises his level of aspiration. Although in the long run he is guided by his ideal goal, which may be rather high, nevertheless his real goal for the next step is kept realistically close to his present position. The unsuccessful individual, on the other hand, tends to show one of two reactions: he sets his goal very low, frequently below his past achievement—that is, he becomes intimidated and gives up reaching out toward higher goals—or he sets his goal far above his ability. This latter conduct is rather common. Sometimes the result is a gesturelike keeping up of high goals without serious striving; it may at other times mean that the individual is following blindly his ideal goal, losing sight of what in the present situation is possible. To develop and to maintain high goals and, at the same time, to keep the plan for the next action realistically within the limits of what is possible, seems to be one of the basic objectives for and a criterion of high morale.

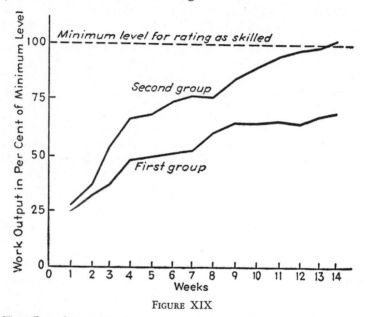

FIGURE XIX

The effect of the level of aspiration and degree of reality of a goal on the achievement of factory workers. Each group contains forty workers. Details of experiment are given in text. (From a study by A. J. Marrow.)

How high a person will set his goal is deeply affected by the standards of the group to which he belongs, as well as by the standards of groups below and above him. Experiments with college students prove that, if the standards of a group are low, an individual will slacken his efforts and set his goals far below those he could reach. He will, on the other hand, raise his goals if the group standards are raised. In other words, both the ideals and the action of an individual depend upon the group to which he belongs and upon the goals and expectations of that group. That the problem of individual morale is to a large extent a social-psychological problem of group goals and group standards is thus clear, even in those fields where the person seems to follow individual rather than group goals. Such a connection between individual and group morale is, of course, still closer in regard to the pursuit of group goals.

An experiment again clarifies the issue. Experiences with sewing-machine workers in a newly erected plant in a rural area of the South demonstrate the manner in which level of aspiration influences learning and achievement in factory work.[2] After a week's training, the output of the novices ranged from 20 per cent to 25 per cent of the quantity accepted as a standard for skilled operators. (See Fig. XIX.) When, nevertheless, the novices were informed that this standard was one which they ought to reach in ten to twelve weeks, the disparity between the level of their performance at the end of the first week and the stated goal was too great —so great, indeed, that the subjects invariably expressed skepticism of ever reaching it. Since the plant was newly organized, there were no skilled workers actually doing the job at the standard speed; hence the goal seemed to be "too difficult," unattainable. Inasmuch as the wage these novices earned was already greater than that to which they were accustomed, there was nothing either outside or inside the plant to give the higher standards social reality for the group. As a result, the individuals were pleased with their progress in spite of the dissatisfaction of the supervisors; improvements were slow, learning plateaus common, and after fourteen weeks only 66 per cent of the standard had been reached.

For a second group of novices who started at the same level, a definite goal was set each week, to be reached at the end of that week, in addition to the information about the general standards. At that time, too, a large number of the older workers in the plant had achieved the standard. This combination of an immediate goal

[2] I am indebted to Dr. Alfred J. Marrow for making these data available.

for the near future and the acceptance of the final goal as a real standard for the group led to a much more rapid improvement on the part of this group of novices. With but few learning plateaus, the average of the group had more than reached the goal standard at the end of the fourteenth week.

MORALE IN THE PURSUIT OF GROUP GOALS AND
TIME PERSPECTIVE

Unfortunately there are few studies available which permit scientific conclusions about the relation between group morale and time perspective. A comparison of groups with democratic and autocratic structures, however, suggests certain conclusions. These groups, for example, showed very striking differences during periods when the leader left. Whereas the work morale of the democratic group was sustained at a high level, that of the autocratic group fell rapidly. In a short time, the latter group ceased entirely to produce. This difference may be traced to the relation between the individual and the group goals and to certain aspects of time perspective.

The organization of work, like any other aspect of the organization of the autocratic group, is based on the leader. It is he who determines the policy of the group; it is he who sets the specific goals of action for the members within the group. That means that the goals of the individual as well as his action as a group member are "induced" by the leader. It is the leader's power-field which keeps the individual going, which determines his work morale, and which makes the group an organized unit. In the democratic group, on the contrary, every member has had a hand in determining the policy of the group; every member has helped to lay out the plans. As a result, each is more "we-centered" and less "ego-centered" than the member of the autocratic group. Because the group goes ahead under its own steam, its work morale does not flag as soon as the power-field of the leader is eliminated.

"Acceptance" of the group goals by the member of the autocratic group means giving in to a superior power and subordinating one's own will. In the democratic group, "acceptance" of the group goal by the member means taking it over and making it one's own goal. The readiness to do so, in the latter case, is partly based on the time perspective of the individual; in the past, that is, he himself has participated in setting up that goal and now he feels his individual responsibility in carrying it through. Not less essential is the difference in time perspective of the members of both groups in regard to planning the future. For the distant future, to be sure, the autocratic leader frequently reveals to his subjects some high, ideal goal. But when it comes to immediate action, it is one of the accepted means of the autocratic leader to reveal to his followers not more than the immediate next step of his actual plans. In this way not only is he able to keep the future of the members in his own hands; in addition he makes the members dependent on him, and he can direct them from moment to moment in whatever direction he wishes.

The member of a democratic group who himself has helped to lay out the long-range plan has a rather different time perspective. In a much clearer situation, he is able to take not only the next step but also the following step quite independently. Because he knows his position and action within the larger group plan, he can modify his own action with the changing situation.

In contrast to both democratic and autocratic groups, the *laissez faire* group, where the leader keeps hands off, shows only sporadic flare-ups of group planning or of long-range individual projects. The work morale of such a group is very low compared with either that of the democratic or the autocratic group—an indication of the importance of definite goals for group morale. Not those goals which can be reached easily but a psychological future with obstacles and high goals is conducive to high morale.

Certain groups in the work camps for conscientious objectors, who as a rule pay for their own upkeep, are frequently permitted to plan by themselves how to reach the work objectives set for them. If reports are correct, these groups, with their self-planned organization, produce many times as much as groups under ordinary methods of supervision. One factor behind this achievement seems to be a long-range time perspective combined with the definiteness of their goal: the conscientious objectors attempt to train for the difficult task of reconstruction in Europe after the war.

LEADERSHIP, MORALE, AND TIME PERSPECTIVE

In an experiment by Bavelas investigating problems of training leaders, the importance of time perspective is apparent, both for the morale of the leaders themselves and for the effect of the leaders in turn on the group morale. The striking change in the morale of the leaders from "low morale" before training to "high morale" after three weeks of training is related to the fact that the goals of these individuals changed from a day-to-day attempt to keep their insecure W.P.A. jobs to a broader—and actually more difficult—less personal goal of giving children the benefit of experiencing genuine democratic group life. Such a change in goal level and time perspective was brought about partly by the experience of membership in a democratic training group which had itself set definite goals and laid out its plans, and partly by the experience of leaving a depressive, narrow, and meaningless past for a future which, with all its uncertainty, contained a goal worth striving toward.

A positive time perspective, a time perspective guided by worth-while goals, is one of the basic elements of high morale. At the same time, the process is reciprocal; high morale itself creates long-range time perspective and sets up worth-while goals. At the end of the training process, the leaders mentioned above had set for themselves goals far above those of which previously they would have dared dream. We are dealing here with one of these circular types of dependencies which are frequently found in social psychology. The highly intelligent person, for example, is better able than the feeble-minded person to create situations which will be easy to handle. As a result, the feeble-minded, with his low ability, frequently finds himself in more difficult situations than the normal. Similarly, the socially maladjusted person creates more difficult social situations for himself than does the well-adjusted person and, doing badly in the difficult situation, easily goes from bad to worse. Again, poor morale makes for a poor time perspective, which in turn results in still poorer morale; whereas high morale sets not only high goals but is likely to create situations of progress conducive to still better morale.

This circular process can be observed also in regard to the morale of the group as a whole. The interdependence among the members of a group, in fact, makes the circularity of the processes even more unmistakable. In one experiment, for instance, a group of children, having been together for one hour in a democratic group, spontaneously demanded the continuation of that group. When informed of the lack of an adult leader, they organized themselves. Their morale, in other words, was high enough to broaden their time perspective; they set themselves a group goal extending over weeks—and later included a half-year project.

REALISM, MORALE, AND TIME PERSPECTIVE

One aspect of time perspective which is essential for morale is realism. Here again we encounter the same paradox as that underlying productivity: one criterion of morale is the height of the goal level which the individual is ready to accept seriously. For high morale, the objective to be reached will represent a great step forward from the present state of affairs. The "realistic" politician who always keeps both feet on the ground and his hand in the pork barrel is a symbol of low morale. On the other hand, the "idealistic" individual who has high ideals without making serious efforts to attain them can likewise make few claims to being a person of high morale. Morale demands both a goal sufficiently above the present state of affairs, and an effort to reach the distant goal through actions planned with sufficient realism to promise an actual step forward. One might say that this paradox—to be realistic, and at the same time be guided by high goals—lies at the heart of the problem of morale, at least as far as time perspective is concerned.

TOO IMMEDIATE AND TOO DISTANT GOALS

What an immediate or a far distant goal means for realism and morale and how it is related to the time perspective of the individual or of a group might best be illustrated by certain aspects of development. The normal healthy child in the elementary school lives in groups of children whose standards and values, whose ideologies and goals, will be of utmost importance for his own goals and his own conduct. If he is fortunate enough to be born in the United States, there will be a good chance that his school group will have a sufficiently democratic atmosphere to give him a clear, first-hand experience in what it means to be a leader as well as a follower in a democratic group, what it means to "play fair," to recognize differences of opinion and differences of ability without intolerance or bossiness and equally, too, without softness or lack of backbone. Only a few children will have experienced anything approaching a perfect democracy; still, they will have experienced frequently a group atmosphere which approaches democracy sufficiently to give them a better taste of democratic procedures than the vast majority of the citizens of European countries are likely ever to have experienced.

Experiments indicate that children at eight years are more altruistic than adults, and that children at ten years are strongly guided by an ideology of fairness. In short, the conduct of the average child at that age follows relatively closely the standards and values of the groups to which he belongs; but these groups are the face-to-face groups of his school, his family, his gang. The period of time to which these standards and goals are related in a realistic manner is a matter of weeks, months, or at most of a few years. The scope of time and space in which national politics takes place in the social world of the adult is, for the young child, something too large and too overpowering to be considered by him in any but a highly abstract or naïve manner.

Growing through adolescence to young manhood or womanhood means enlarging the scope and the time perspective of one's psychological world. In a measure, it means also leaving the small face-to-face groups, such as the family, or else assigning these small groups a secondary place in a larger social world with which the young person now seriously has to come into grips. It is the eternal right of every young generation to consider critically the standards and values of this larger world of the older generation. The better and the more democratic the education during childhood has been, the more serious and the more honest will these critical considerations be.

For the young person growing into problems of such magnitude —in fact, for anybody facing for the first time problems of a new order of magnitude—two reactions are typical. The individual may, in the first place, shrink from making decisions of such importance, trying rather to restrict himself to the smaller time perspective which he was just outgrowing. His low morale will then lead him to place his main emphasis on the small day-to-day goals. An example is the college girl who, because she is so disgusted with the war "over there in Europe," will not even look at the newspapers or listen to the radio.[3]

At the other extreme is the individual who refuses to think in a time perspective of less than a thousand years. He thinks in terms of "what ought to be"; his goals as such are frequently excellent, and he refuses to take any action which might run counter to his principles. In so far as his goals are characterized by a high discrepancy between "what is" and "what should be," between the wish level for the future and the present reality level, his time perspective is opposite to that of an individual who is satisfied with the status quo. But the very weight which the distant goal has for the individual who takes it seriously, the very fact that he is dissatisfied with the present situation, make it difficult for him to give sufficient consideration to the actual structure of the present situation, or to conceive realistically what step in the present world can be taken to achieve this end. For one growing into problems which deal with a new scope of time perspective, it is difficult, at first, to distinguish between the cynic, who is ready to use any means to his ends, and the person of high morale, who takes his goal seriously enough to do what is necessary to change the present state of affairs.

TWO FOUNDATIONS OF ACTION

The conviction that a certain action will lead toward the direction in which the individual wants to go and not in just the opposite direction is based partly on what is called technical

[3] See postscript to this chapter.

knowledge. But for the individual this knowledge is limited; his actions are always based, in part, on some type of "belief." There are many types of such beliefs on which the principle of realism within morale can be based. We shall mention but two.

The exigencies of modern warfare have compelled the armies to give a fair measure of independence to the individual private. In some respects, the army of Nazi Germany can be said to have more status-democracy between officers and men than had previously existed in the army of the Kaiser. On the whole, however, and particularly in regard to civilian life and to civilian education, Hitler has placed the relation between leader and led on a basis of blind obedience to a degree unheard of in modern life outside of certain monasteries. Ever since Hitler came to power, the nursery school teacher, for example, has been instructed never to explain an order to a child, even if he could understand the reason, because the child should learn to obey blindly. "There are many things which can be forgiven, no matter how evil they may be. But disloyalty to the Fuehrer can never be pardoned."

The belief that one's action goes in the correct direction is, in such an atmosphere, based primarily if not exclusively on the trust in the leader. The area in which independent thinking is permitted is small, more or less limited to the execution of the immediate next step as objective. Blind obedience means abandoning, in all essential areas, that measure of reasoning and independent judgment which prevailed in Germany before Hitler's rise to power and which, to a much greater extent, has been one of the traditional rights of the citizen in the United States.

It is not chance that the fight against reason and the replacement of reason by sentiment has been one of the unfailing symptoms of politically reactionary movements throughout the centuries. To recognize reason socially means that a sound argument "counts," no matter who brings it forth; it means recognizing the basic equality of men. In an autocracy, only the leader needs to be correctly informed; in a democracy, popular determination of policy can work only if the people who participate in goal-setting are realistically aware of the actual situation. In other words, the emphasis on truth, the readiness to let the people know about difficult situations and failures, does not spring merely from an abstract "love of truth" but is rather a political necessity. Here lies one of the points on which democratic morale can, in the long run, be superior to authoritarian morale. A far more stable ground for morale than the belief in the ability of any leader individually is truth itself.

POSTSCRIPT

This chapter was written before December 7, 1941; now we are at war. The effect on the morale of the country has been immediate and striking—a circumstance which bears out some of the points we have discussed.

The attack on Hawaii has shown that Japan represents a much more serious danger than many had thought. But this feeling of increased and close danger has heightened rather than depressed morale, being as it is in line with the general finding that morale changes, not parallel with, but rather, inversely to the amount of difficulty, so long as certain goals are maintained.

The experience of attack upon our own country has overnight brought war down from the cloudy realms of possibility to the level of reality. Although the college girl whom we mentioned above may still be far from realizing fully what it means to be at war, nonetheless war is no longer something "over there in Europe." It is here. Thus as a result of our being in the war, the will to win has become a clear and unquestioned objective.

Before December 7, what was a realistic outlook for one individual was doubted by a second and ridiculed as impossible by a third. Now the situation has been clarified. Countless conflicts, whether among factions in the population or within each individual himself, have ceased now that the major aspects of the time perspectives are definitely set.

Being within this new and definite situation means that certain basic goals and necessary actions are "given." In such a situation no special effort is required to keep morale high. The very combination of a definite objective, the belief in final success, and the realistic facing of great difficulties *is* high morale. The individual who makes extreme efforts and accepts great risks for worth-while goals does not feel that he is making a sacrifice; instead, he merely feels that he is acting naturally.

When a major decision has been made, it frequently happens that the individual or the group will show high morale in the new situation because of a sudden clear awareness of the objectives of the enterprise as a whole. As the effort proceeds, however, a variety of detailed problems and difficulties is bound to arise and to occupy a more prominent position. There is danger that groups which started out with enthusiasm may yet lose their "punch" when the clearness of the situation at the time of decision has been clouded by such a multitude of details, problems, and immediate difficulties. Group morale during a prolonged effort depends much on the degree to which the members keep clearly in view the total task and the final objective.

In the months and years to come, then, civilian morale can be expected to depend much upon the clarity and the value of our war goals, and upon the degree to which such values come to be deeply rooted within each individual.

8

THE SOLUTION OF A CHRONIC CONFLICT IN INDUSTRY

(1944)

THE purpose of a case study is to describe and analyze an individual incident. Seldom can this analysis be used as proof of a theory. However, it may illustrate the interdependence of some underlying factors and help us to see certain general problems.

The following case study of conflict in a factory is presented as an illustration of certain aspects of group dynamics and theoretical interpretation. The case involves a long-smoldering conflict that has periodically flared out but has always been patched up.

The incident did not take longer than one afternoon—1:30 to 5:00 P.M. The psychologist who handled the matter considers it a routine case and only reluctantly agreed to write an account of it. The author (although feeling that a neat job has been done) does not doubt that similar solutions are brought about by good management in many factories.

The story is part of a larger research project undertaken by Alex Bavelas and will be presented as he has written it, namely, as a sequence of acts, each containing a number of scenes.

The Characters: Paulson, the mechanic; Sulinda, the supervisor; Alanby, the boss; Bavelas, the psychologist and narrator; machine operators (girls).

The Setting: A sewing factory employing about 170 operators, five floor-girls, one supervisor and one mechanic.

ACT I. SCENE 1

One afternoon as I was returning to my office, I happened to look into the boss's office as I walked by and saw Paulson and Sulinda standing in front of his desk. All three were obviously painfully ill at ease and I surmised something was wrong.

I was not surprised, therefore, to be summoned by the boss almost immediately. "You're just the man we've been waiting for" were his first words; the other two merely looked more uncomfortable. I made some trifling joking remark and lit a cigarette to gain a little time. I offered cigarettes; only the boss accepted one. I sat on a corner of his desk but this did not noticeably break the rigid atmosphere. "Well, what's going on?" I directed the remark to the boss because although I needed information I saw by now that Paulson and Sulinda had quarrelled and I did not want to risk asking either of them.

ACT I. SCENE 2

The boss explained that Paulson and Sulinda were having some trouble because they did not agree on which machines should be repaired first and that one of the operators was playing them against each other by gossiping with each about the other. At this Sulinda's eyes watered and I was surprised to see Paulson too on the verge of tears. I remarked that such behavior by an operator was quite common and mentioned its occurrence in another factory where I had worked. I pointed out that what was said by whom was not so important as the amount of hurt it could cause people if they took it seriously, and that things got so twisted about after a few repetitions from one person to the other it was hopeless to find out exactly what had been meant by the original remark. I then looked at my watch and remarked that I had made a short appointment with an operator whom I had to meet immediately, but that it would take only a few minutes and I wanted to talk over this thing in detail with each of them and with the girl. I tried to give the impression that I felt the gossiping operator to be the root of the trouble.

ACT I. SCENE 3

Turning to Sulinda I asked her if she would be too busy to see me right after that appointment; if she was, could I see her later that afternoon.   I added that I knew she was probably needed upstairs right away. She answered that she could see me any time and we agreed that I would see her right after my interview with the operator. Then turning to Paulson I asked him if I could talk with him in his machine shop. He said it would be O.K.

ACT I.   SCENE 4

I walked upstairs to the shop with Sulinda. She started by saying that what got her mad was Paulson telling lies about her and the girl's trying to make a liar of her right to her face. I responded by saying I could understand just how such an incident must make her feel, having been involved once in a similar situation. I could also see how the whole thing might be a misunderstanding. Without allowing further conversation along that line I went on to my "appointment."

ACT I.   SCENE 5

In the next few minutes I interviewed the boss who had no more information to offer but who told me that I came in just as Sulinda was getting ready to "walk out" and that Paulson also was saying that he was quitting. The boss hoped that I could smooth things over, saying that although this kind of thing happened every now and then, this time it was worse. In his opinion the trouble was caused because Paulson was too independent and Sulinda lost her temper too easily— the whole thing growing out of a mutual dislike that had always existed.

[The reader may have noticed that the psychologist has quickly succeeded in getting the supervisor and the mechanic out of their overcoats, the one back to his machine shop, the other to her floor.]

ACT II.

In the interview with Sulinda, she described the situation as follows: Paulson was not a very good mechanic to start with. Often he didn't know what was wrong with a machine and would tinker around for ages and when he got through it would still not be right. He would blame the operator for mishandling the machine or say that the thread was no good or make other excuses.

According to Sulinda, a girl had come to her that afternoon and said that Paulson refused to fix her machine. She went to Paulson and told him he would have to do it and that the girl had told her he refused to fix it. At this he got very angry and said he had said no such thing. He went to the girl and asked her why she had told Sulinda that he had said he would not fix her machine when he had merely said that he would do it later. The operator answered that she had not told Sulinda that at all and Sulinda was lying. Thereupon, Paulson and the operator went to Sulinda and confronted her with what amounted to proof that she had lied to Paulson. Sulinda at once got her coat and went down to tell the boss she was quitting. The boss heard her story and summoned Paulson.

[The girls who work under Sulinda depend mainly on her but also depend on Paulson for machine repair. It is the problem of Paulson's and Sulinda's authority which has made the lie such an important issue. For Sulinda, acknowledging the lie would mean losing face and might seriously weaken her position with the girls. In addition, Sulinda was particularly hurt because what the girl considered to be a "lie" was an action which Sulinda obviously had done for the sake of this very girl; she wanted the girl not to lose time and money by waiting for the repair. For Paulson the issue involved a threat to his honor, to his position of authority with the girls and to his status of equality with Sulinda.]

ACT III.   SCENE 1

I began asking Sulinda factual questions about the frequency of breakdowns and whether they were more frequent in certain types of machines, etc. After some discussion it became clear that Paulson was kept very busy trying to keep all 170 machines in continuous operation and Sulinda agreed that if he had plenty of time instead of being rushed many sources of irritation would be removed. I asked whether she thought it would help if those girls were interviewed and their attitude on the problem determined. She was sure that I should talk with them because the girls she had mentioned were always complaining and were causing other girls to take the same attitude. I told Sulinda that I would do so and asked if she would like to know what the girls said. She said she would. I ended the interview by remarking that I thought she was quite correct in attributing a large measure of the irritation between mechanic and girls to the overcrowded time schedule of the mechanic and commended her for so objective an attitude.

ACT III. SCENE 2

Next, I interviewed Paulson. Paulson started by explaining how hard he had to work and that he had only one pair of hands and could work only on one machine at a time. After easing the situation with a joke or two, I found it easy to arrive with Paulson at the point of attributing the irritation largely to the impatience of the girls and the scarcity of mechanic-time. He, too, thought that I should talk to the girls and that it would help to know just what they thought. He was especially interested to know what they thought of him as an individual.

[The interview with the mechanic follows a somewhat similar pattern to the interview with the supervisor. Like Sulinda, Paulson's perception of the situation had been dominated by the aspect "right or wrong"; he had regarded Sulinda as being in the wrong, himself in the right. Again the interviewer is able to lead Paulson to a perception of the objective situation. The insufficiency of mechanic-time is stressed but this time the natural irritation of the girls is somewhat more emphasized.

This attempt to change perception by an "action interview" (as distinguished from a mere "fact-finding interview") is one of the basic elements of treatment. By reorienting Sulinda's and Paulson's perception from the field of personal emotional relationship to the same field of "objective" facts, the life-spaces which guide the action of these persons have become more similar although the persons themselves are not yet aware of this similarity.

A few additional points may be mentioned:

(a) The interviewer does not restructure Paulson's and Sulinda's views by "giving" them the facts although such "induction" of the same cognitive structure would probably have been possible. Instead, Paulson and Sulinda are themselves encouraged to look at the objective situation and, therefore, "accept" it to a higher degree as "facts." This procedure does not work out fully with Sulinda.

(b) Being sensitive to power relations, Bavelas is careful to get the consent of Sulinda before approaching the girls under her authority. Sulinda is glad to give it because the trouble-makers have been a threat to her. In this way, definite progress is made in several aspects. Bavelas can approach the girls with the full backing of the supervisor's authority. By asking Sulinda whether she would like him to report back to her he prepares the next action. The action takes on the character of a co-operative endeavor and establishes a good tie between Bavelas and Sulinda. Sulinda becomes, thus, actively involved in the planning of the actions and should, therefore, be more ready to identify herself later on with a proposed solution.

(c) The same procedure is followed with Paulson with slight variations. Bavelas is careful to give attention to Paulson's special motives. For instance, Bavelas accepts immediately Paulson's wish to learn whether the girls like him. By co-operating closely with the mechanic and the supervisor both become parties of the same plan although, in this stage, only factually and not as the result of a co-operative decision.]

ACT III.   SCENE 3

I then called each of the girls in for a short interview. I asked them if they felt that there was insufficient coverage on machine repair. They all agreed that Paulson was O.K. but that he was too busy to do a proper job. I asked each girl if it would be a good idea to get all the girls who were having the most trouble together and see if something couldn't be worked out to reduce the amount of time they had to lose waiting for repairs. They were all eager for some action of this type.

ACT IV.   SCENE 1

The girls were called in as a group and I presented the problem. All of them agreed, as did Sulinda and Paulson, that at certain times when more than one machine broke down there was a shortage of mechanic services. Since it was unlikely that another mechanic would be hired in view of the difficulty of deferring even Paulson from military service, the question was how the services of the one mechanic that we had could most efficiently be used. I proceeded to stimulate group discussion as to the fairest action in each of the following situations: when one machine broke down; when two machines broke down at the same time but neither was more critical than the other in terms of throwing more girls out of work; when more than one machine broke down and one was more important in this respect.

The group discussion resulted in the following plan: (1) When machines had no differential in importance, the rule would be "first come, first served." (2) When there was a difference in machine importance, the most critical machine would be serviced first. (3) That this plan would be presented to Paulson and Sulinda and I would report to the group what they said.

[The accomplishments thus far may be summarized as follows:

1. The mechanic and the supervisor who were ready to leave are back in the plant.
2. The perception of all three fighting parties—the mechanic, the supervisor and the most critical, active group, the operators—who had been preoccupied with the issue of the "lie" and prestige has been turned toward the objective difficulties of production.
3. Without any direct contact between the three parties, it has been established that their views of the production difficulties agree to a reasonable extent.
4. All individuals involved have freely and without pressure expressed their agreement to some future steps.
5. All three parties are in good and friendly rapport with the psychologist.

The procedure of the psychologist is based on the hypothesis that the permanent conflict is at least partly the result of some faulty organization of production. Therefore, before a remedy can be found the production procedure has to be analyzed realistically and sufficiently deeply to lay open the source of the difficulty.

The group lowest in the factory hierarchy is made the foundation for the fact-finding, probably because these operators are most immediately affected and should be most realistically aware of at least some aspects of the problem. Then too, since the operators have a lower position in the factory hierarchy any rule suggested by the authorities, or even a view presented by them as a "fact," is likely to be felt by the operators as something of an imposition. To gain their wholehearted co-operation later on it seems best to start the detailed fact-finding here, and it is also necessary to have the first suggestions for the new rules of production worked out by this group.

Not all the operators but only those who did the most complaining were consulted. This seems strange if one considers that those operators who have less inclination for "trouble-making" are likely to give a more objective picture of the situation. The trouble-makers were made the cornerstone of the investigation since they are particularly important for the group dynamics in the factory. Furthermore, if those operators who usually did not make trouble were to initiate a solution, the trouble-makers would probably resist, feeling that they had been first left out and later pushed into something.

The psychologist as leader of the group discussion presents the problem as an objective question of production procedure. The fact that he has no difficulty in holding the group's attention on this aspect of the situation indicates that the preliminary interviews have set the stage for this perception.

The group discussion discloses that the difficulties are part of the problem of production under war conditions. That these facts emerge through group rather than individual discussion has a number of important advantages. As a rule, group discussion brings out a richer, better balanced, and more detailed picture of the situation. The atmosphere of openness which is possible in group discussion as opposed to the secrecy so characteristic of individual information giving is very important for the readiness to co-operate.

The rules emerging from the discussion were supposed to solve an objective production problem. Impersonal facts rather than power conflicts determine the action in certain situations. These rules are identical with what is required for maximum production output by the factory. The psychologist could have asked the girls what sequence of repair was best for production. The girls would probably have set up the same rules but they would have felt that they were doing something "for the Boss," their motivation being "generosity" or patriotism. The psychologist did not follow this line but asked for a solution on the basis of fairness. This is a matter of relationships between the girls and, since it also involved the question of losing money, it was very close to their self-interest. To have "fairness" the guiding principle for the rules of social conduct in a group is doubtless one of the strongest motives in the American culture.

Since the rules are developed by the girls themselves, their acceptance is implied and strongly entrenched.

Two problems remain: first, acceptance of the rules by the rest of the operators and by the authorities, Sulinda and Paulson; and second, determination of the persons who will be in charge of the execution of the rules.]

ACT IV. SCENE 2

I reported back to Paulson, laying heavy emphasis on the fact that the girls had nothing against him personally; on the contrary they felt that he had more of a job than one mechanic could do. I showed him the girls' plan and his comment was that was exactly what he wanted if only "everybody" would stop trying to order him around. I told him that there was no reason why he should be bothered with making the decisions about which machine was more important at any given time. He was a mechanic and he should be left free of that responsibility. In this he agreed very strongly. I suggested that Sulinda was the one who should take the responsibility of deciding what would have to come first, and the girls could battle it out with her if they didn't like her decisions. In this he also agreed but doubted that Sulinda would like it. I told him that I would see her and that I thought she would be glad to do it if he wouldn't misinterpret her actions as giving orders.

[The psychologist approaches the mechanic first. Paulson's fears are relieved when the psychologist emphasizes at the beginning of the interview that the girls have nothing against him. It makes Paulson feel good and more ready to view the situation objectively. In this atmosphere he finds it easy to agree.

The rest of the interview is dominated by the psychologist's endeavor to solve vital aspects for permanent solution of the conflict. Such a permanent solution requires that a correct set-up be established from the point of view of production, and that the authorities have definite objectives in mind and do not conflict. In our case, the conflict was based on the overlapping authority in the field of repair. Now rules are found and responsibilities assigned.

The psychologist feels that the only sensible and stable procedure would be to have the supervisor in charge of determining the order in which the machines should be repaired since it is her (and not the mechanic's) responsibility to keep up maximum production.

The method by which Bavelas presents the problem to the mechanic follows the same principle which was used in the preceding scene with the operators: The reality is presented correctly, but those aspects are brought into the fore which are linked with the psychological situation of the person in question and are helpful in bringing about favorable permanent motivation. Rather than speak of dividing authority, the psychologist points to the possibility of getting rid of the burden of making decisions and taking responsibility which is actually not the mechanic's job.

That this was a correct and realistic approach is clear if we consider somewhat more closely the situation which the mechanic faced whenever more than one machine needed repair. To Paulson, the shop is an agreeable place, a kind of sanctuary where he is his own boss as long as he has something to do. He has tried to stay in that area as much as possible. When he has to enter the floor for repair work he is on "foreign soil" which is under the authority of the supervisor. If three machines are out of order, the mechanic is in a conflict situation resulting from the forces corresponding to his own wish to repair all three machines. Each of these forces points in a different direction. Parallel forces, induced by the various operators, exist in these different directions, the strength of each force depending somewhat on the clamoring of the operator. In addition, there is the force induced by the supervisor who may either leave the mechanic to guess what she wants or may express a definite preference.

This situation is typical of a decision situation providing the possibility of high emotional tension for two reasons: (a) the restraining forces against the decision must be considerable because any wrong decision is likely to bring about trouble with the operator and supervisor; and (b) cognitively the field is unstructured when the mechanic does not know whether repairing one or the other machine first will lead him into the most trouble.

These factors together made the decision situation most disagreeable to Paulson, so much so that not only did the particular moment of decision have a negative valence but also the fact of being on the floor. Consequently the mechanic is very eager to accept any measure which offers hope of leading him out of this painful situation.

It may be pointed out that the presentation of the problem to Paulson by the psychologist is not designed to "trick" the mechanic into an agreement (and place him under the authority of the supervisor). The presentation by the psychologist is in line with the facts. The new plan sets up definite general rules on an objective basis in regard to what ought to be done. Someone will have to do the fact-finding in each individual situation. Someone has to decide in case of doubt which sequence of repair would waste a minimum of operator hours. But this is all that has to be decided by the supervisor. She is not free to tell the mechanic arbitrarily what he shall do. In fact, she is not supposed to give him orders. All that she can do is pass certain information about the relative importance of machines on to him. On the basis of this information, he will follow the rules readily agreed upon by everyone. The psychologist stresses this point in his final remark to avoid misconception which would hurt the mechanic's pride.

On the whole Scene 2 is short and proceeds smoothly toward a full acceptance of the new plan by the mechanic. His doubt that Sulinda would agree is evidence that the tension between them has not fully disappeared. It indicates, in addition, that the mechanic does not feel that he himself will get the worst of the bargain.]

Act IV.   Scene 3

I showed the girls' plan to Sulinda and she thought that it was exactly what should be done, adding that she had been trying to do it but no one could tell Paulson anything. I told her that Paulson would be ready to accept her decision on priority of repairs to be done. I also indicated that the girls seemed ready to co-operate on such a plan. She was ready to try it, however, although she was skeptical.

The discussion with Sulinda shows a pattern similar to that with Paulson. She accepts the plan readily as something she has always wished for. She can hardly believe that Paulson would be ready to accept her "decision on prerogatives," thereby indicating that she does not feel she is giving up power. On the other hand, it is made clear by the psychologist that her judgment will be limited to decision of the sequence of repairs.

Act IV.   Scenes 4-6

Scene 4. I told Paulson that Sulinda liked the plan and was ready to try it.

Scene 5. Then I called the girls back for a short meeting in which we reviewed the plan and went over the procedure carefully.

Scene 6. After that I reported to Sulinda and Paulson that the arrangements had been concluded and would go into effect and that any ideas would be welcome.

[The last scenes are very short. Each of the parties—the mechanic, the supervisor, and the operators—is informed that all the other parties agree to the arrangement and that the new procedure will go into effect immediately. The psychologist is careful to stress his readiness to welcome new ideas. This is a kind of safety valve for later changes which may seem desirable.]

Epilogue

A few weeks later the boss asked me if I had noticed a change in Paulson. I said I had not. He went on to explain that Paulson seemed to have much less work to do and plenty of time to tinker around. His relations with Sulinda were better than they had ever been and there had been no more conflict with the girls. A week or so later, Paulson at his own expense and using his own equipment installed a system of loudspeakers in the factory and played recorded music two periods a day. The whole shop enjoyed this and relations became even more pleasant.

Three months after this incident—during which time no new difficulties arose—a third party had an interview with the mechanic.

This report reads:

Paulson estimates that repairs are a third less now than before; where he now gets an average of 10 calls a day, he previously got 15 or 20. He believes the chief decrease has come in the number of trivial calls; the number of genuine repairs is about the same. He blames the former excessive number of trivial calls on "agitation"—"the girls just wanted to make trouble." Paulson also remarked that there had been a decrease in agitation against Sulinda.

When asked "how come?" Paulson said—"I think the music had a lot to do with it," referring to the loudspeaker system he had installed. This made the girls more friendly. Bavelas' being there had also helped. He talked to some of the girls, showed Sulinda's side of the picture and explained what things were to be expected and accepted.

One change helped to decrease the general agitation. Somehow there was an impression that Sulinda and Paulson were enemies when actually, off the job, they were the best of friends. In the factory, "Well, we bickered back and forth but everybody does it and we thought nothing of it. But they got the impression we hated each other." In consequence, some of the girls attempted to stir up trouble. When it was understood that there was no enmity between Paulson and Sulinda, the girls realized they were no longer vulnerable and a lot of the agitation ceased.

On the whole, then, it seems that the brief treatment has actually solved a chronic conflict. It has established good relations in a previously fighting triangle, the mechanic, the supervisor, and the operators. Finally, it has led to an unexpected diminishing of repairs in the factory.

It seems that the basic principles which guided the action of the psychologist might be summed up as follows: *The realistic*

demands of production have to be satisfied in a way which con-
forms with the nature of group dynamics.

To bring about a permanent solution it does not suffice to create amicable relations. The conflict described arose out of an aspect of production where overlapping authorities existed in a cognitively unclear situation. The procedure is guided to an equal degree by the consideration of production and the problem of social relations.

As to details, one might mention the following points. The factory work can be seen as a process in which the speed is determined by certain driving and restraining forces. The production process runs through certain "channels" as determined by the physical and social setting, particularly by certain "rules" and by the authorities in power (management). To increase production one can try to increase the driving forces by higher incentives or pressure, or try to weaken those forces that keep production down. The procedure described here follows the latter possibility. It tries to eliminate certain conflicts within the group and certain psychological forces acting on a key individual (the mechanic) which deter his efforts.

The attempt for a lasting improvement is based on a study of the present situation in regard to a certain portion (machine repair) of the production channel. By setting up new rules and regulations, the production channels are modified objectively.

Even the best plan of reorganizing production channels is worthless if it does not fit the human beings who have to live and react in that setting. The procedure described is therefore heavily influenced by consideration of group dynamics. Indeed, every step is influenced by this aspect.

It is important that even the first step of fact-finding, which easily might be viewed as a scientific task for an expert rather than a social act itself, is imbedded in a social procedure. It is one of the outstanding characteristics of this case (and seems to be typical of the methods used by this psychologist) that the fact-finding itself is made the cornerstone for the change.

The choice of the operators as a main fact-finding body may

have been influenced by the fact that they are nearest to the production problem. If one intends to create a general friendly atmosphere of co-operation rather than a straight authoritarian system, if one wants to gain full co-operation, the lowest group should do the planning for the first step, since they would regard any other action as an attempt to make them agree to a procedure set up by the authorities. On the other hand, the person in position of authority, like the mechanic or the supervisor, will not have the same reaction when asked to agree to a plan first developed by the operators because being in the position of authority they can reject it.

That the fact-finding is based on only part of the operators might be merely the outcome of the factors discussed before. Perhaps it would have been better to include the other operators. At least, for adequacy of fact-finding and co-operation of the machine operators it sufficed to have the most troublesome part of that group involved. Even the definition of a "fact" for this type of treatment has the two aspects of production and of group dynamics. It is correct that a "sufficiently objective" picture of the production channels and problems should arise from the investigation. But it is equally essential to realize that the "subjective" view of the participants counts most.

In addition to establishing the facts, fact-finding has two more important functions in this treatment. Fact-finding is one of the best means of changing the dimensions along which the *perception* of the individual proceeds. It is probably correct to state that *the action of an individual depends directly on the way in which he perceives the situation*. One can propose the theory that whether a change of ideas or values does or does not affect the action of an individual depends upon whether or not his perception is changed. The correctness of this theory seems to be suggested by the experience in rather divergent fields, including those of stuttering and psychopathology. One of the main characteristics of this method is to change action by changing perception.

Fact-finding in this method is consciously used as a first step of action. The psychologist's or expert's knowing the facts does not have any influence unless these data are "accepted as facts" by the group members. Here lies a particular advantage of making the fact-finding a group endeavor. Coming together to discuss the facts and set up a plan is already an endeavor in co-operative action. It goes a long way to establish the atmosphere of co-operation, openness, and confidence toward which this procedure strives. Although the mechanic and the supervisor do not participate directly in the group discussion of the operators, we have seen that the psychologist was very careful to involve them actively in the total scheme of fact-finding and planning.

It has been emphasized already that group meetings are not considered a panacea. They are carefully prepared by steps which take into consideration the psychological situation of the individual, although the individual is considered at every step in his position in the total group. These individual considerations are along two lines. First, the motivation for a change in perception and action is based, as much as possible, on realistic judgment of the person's own situation. Second, much is done to lower the general level of emotionality during each step in the procedure. Wherever possible the individual is praised; his feeling of insecurity or anxiety is eased (Paulson and the girls); everything is done to have the persons appear in a good light to each other without becoming unrealistic. As a rule this lowering of emotionality is attempted by indirect means. One example is the way in which the polarization of the conflict with one operator (lie issue) is depersonalized by bringing up the problems of the group of trouble-makers. It is clear that in this way the issue becomes less personal and at the same time is bent to an objective group question by having this one girl disappear into the group.

It might be worthwhile to note that the original issue—namely, the lie and the resulting threat of quitting by the mechanic and the supervisor—seems to have evaporated into thin air without ever having been treated directly. It seems that with a change in perception of the situation from that of a power problem to that of factory production, the lie issue, in the beginning a hard fact blocking smooth-running factory life, has lost the character of a "fact." This itself can be taken as a symptom of how deep and real the change of the perception and the psychological situation of all parties concerned has been.

PART III. INTER-GROUP CONFLICTS
AND GROUP BELONGINGNESS

9

PSYCHO-SOCIOLOGICAL PROBLEMS
OF A MINORITY GROUP

(1935)

THE high sensitivity persons show to any change which may possibly affect their security can to some extent be ascribed to fear of being unable to earn a living, yet this sensitivity is probably connected with something even more fundamental than the fear of hunger.

Every action one performs has some specific "background," and is determined by that background. A statement or a gesture which may be quite appropriate between companions in a swimming pool may be out of place, even insulting, at a dinner party. Judgment, understanding, perception are impossible without a related background, and the meaning of every event depends directly upon the nature of its background.

Experiments have shown how important the background is for any perception. They have also proved that the background itself is not often perceived, but only the "figure" or "event." Similarly, all actions are based on the ground the person happens to stand upon. The firmness of his actions and the clearness of his decisions depend largely upon the stability of this "ground," although he himself may not even be aware of its nature. Whatever a person does or wishes to do, he must have some "ground" to stand upon. This is probably the primary reason why he is extremely affected the moment this ground begins to give way.

One of the most important constituents of the ground on which the individual stands is the social group to which he "belongs." In the case of a child growing up in a family, the family-group often makes up his main ground. We know that instability of the background in childhood may lead to an instability of the adult. It generally requires a strong conflict for a child not to be clear about his belonging or not belonging to a group.

One of the basic characteristics of belonging is that the same individual generally belongs to many groups. For instance, a person (p) may belong economically to the upper middle class ($uMCl$) —perhaps he is a prosperous merchant. He may be a member of a small family (F) of three persons, which is part of a larger family group (lF), and which may be concentrated in a few towns in the East. This larger family group may be the third American generation of Irish ancestry (I_3G). Politically the man may be a Republican (Rep). Religiously he may be a Catholic and may have some leading position in his church group. He may also be the Secretary of the Northeastern Division of Elks (E).

Fig. XX represents the sociological situation by means of topology: a group the person belongs to is represented as a "region" of which the person is a part. The different groups ($A, B, C \ldots$) to which the same person (p) belongs can be related in either of two ways. The one group (A) may be a sub-group of the other (B), e.g., the two groups F and lF; or both groups may overlap, e.g., lF and E.

During most of his life the adult acts not purely as an individual but as a member of a social group. However, the different groups a person belongs to are not all equally important at a given moment. Sometimes his belonging to one group is dominant, sometimes his belonging to another. He may, for instance, in one situation feel and act as a member of his political group; at other times as a member of his family, religious, or business group. Generally, in every situation the person seems to know what group he belongs to and to what group he does not belong. He knows more or less clearly where he stands, and this position largely determines his behavior.

Neverthelesss there are occasions when his belonging to a

group is doubtful or not clear for the individual. For example, a person entering a gathering may for a moment doubt whether he belongs there. Or, to take an example of a less momentary situation, a newcomer in a club may for a period of months feel uncertain as to whether or not he is accepted. This unclearness of the situation, this uncertainty about the ground upon which he is acting, leads generally to uncertainty in behavior. The

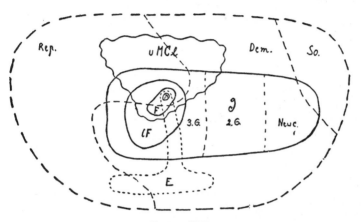

FIGURE XX

p, person	*3.G*, third generation in U. S. A.
F, family	*uMCl*, upper middle class
lF, larger family	*Rep*, Republicans
I, Irish American	*Dem*, Democrats
Newc, newcomer	*So*, Socialists
2.G, second generation in U. S. A.	*E*, Elks

person does not feel at home and will therefore be more or less self-conscious, inhibited, or inclined to over-act.

In both examples, the uncertainty of belonging is due to the fact that the individual is crossing the margin of one group into another (coming from an outer group to the gathering or to the club).

There are persons whose whole life-situation is characterized by such uncertainty about their belonging, resulting from standing near a margin of groups. This is typical, for instance, of the *nouveaux riches* or of other persons crossing the margin of social classes. It is typical furthermore of members of religious or national minority groups everywhere who try to enter the main group.

It is characteristic of individuals crossing the margin between social groups that they are not only uncertain about their belonging to the group they are ready to enter, but also about their belonging to the group they are leaving. It is for example one of the greatest theoretical and practical difficulties of the Jewish problem that Jewish people are often, in a high degree, uncertain of their relation to the Jewish group. They are uncertain whether they actually belong to the Jewish group, in what respect they belong to this group, and in what degree.

One reason that an individual finds it difficult to comprehend whether and in what respect he belongs to the Jewish group is the general fact of the manifold overlapping of the groups one belongs to. No doubt, even for a Jew who is highly conscious of being a Jew, there are as for everybody, many social groups to which he belongs. There are many situations in which the group which dominates his actions is not the Jewish group. As in our example of the Irishman, the Jewish store-keeper acts, and has to act frequently as a member of a business group, as a member of a special family, or as a member of a club. He may, for instance, act as a member of his family against a member of another Jewish family or against a Jew belonging to some other business group.

There exists a natural relation between the character of a given situation and the character of the group which dominates the be-havior of the individual in this situation. In different situations different feelings of belonging should be predominant. If an individual always acts as a member of the same specific group, it is usually symptomatic of the fact that he is somewhat out of balance, for he does not respond naturally and freely to the demands of the present situation. He feels too strongly his membership in a certain group, and this indicates that his personal relationship to this group is not sound.

One can observe behavior in certain Jewish individuals which is the result of such an exaggerated consciousness of belonging to the Jewish group. This over-emphasis is only a different form of expression of the same kind of relationship which, in other individuals, leads to an under-emphasis. There are persons who, in a situation in which it would be natural to respond as Jews, do not respond so; they repress or conceal their Jewishness.

The overlapping of the many social groups to which the same individual belongs is one of the main reasons why many individuals ask themselves again and again whether it is necessary to maintain their membership in the Jewish group. They often think that they no longer belong to the group, especially if they endeavor to avoid the disagreeable facts connected with this membership.

Among the members of minorities or other social groups which are not in fortunate positions, there are single individuals or larger sections of the group which see their main hope in crossing the line that separates their group from the others. They may hope to cross the line individually or to destroy it entirely. One speaks in this connection of a tendency for "assimilation." It is worthwhile to ask how this tendency of the individual is related to the situation of his group and his position within the group.

Since the Jews live in Diaspora, the Jewish group is in all nations numerically a minority group. That means that they comprise a relatively small part within a larger social body. The character of the group is furthermore determined by the strength of the boundary which separates this group from the other groups, and by the character of this boundary. Furthermore the degree of similarity or dissimilarity of both groups is important.

The strength and the character of the boundary of the Jewish group has changed a great deal in the course of history. In the period of the Ghetto, there were clear, strong boundaries between the Jewish groups and the other groups. The fact that the Jews then had to live in restricted territories or towns of the country, and in certain districts within the town, made the boundaries obvious and unquestionable for everybody (Fig. XXI).

At least for certain hours of the day, the Ghetto wall separated this group entirely from communication with other social groups.

Besides these physical restrictions there were social boundaries which varied to some degree for the different individuals of the group, but which were generally deep and were strictly observed by both sides, by the Jews and by the non-Jews.

One of the most important facts for all social life is probably the amount of what one may call "space of free movement." The boundaries of the Ghetto imposed a strict limitation for the "bodily locomotion" of the Jews. A similarly strong restriction limited their "social locomotions." There were many occupations

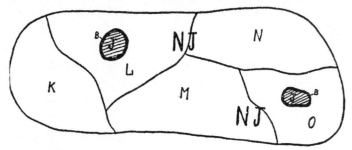

FIGURE XXI

J, Jewish group
NJ, non-Jewish group
B, barrier between Jewish and non-Jewish groups
K.L.M.N.O. . . . may represent geographical areas or occupational fields

As we cannot make use of colors here, we may indicate the degree of similarity between groups by representing the non-Jewish groups as empty regions, the Jewish groups in the Ghetto period as regions with narrow hatching, and the emancipated Jewish groups (Fig. XXII) as regions with wide hatching.

not open to Jews, which means, if we represent all possible occupations as one totality of regions, that the social space of free movement was limited to comparatively few parts of this totality.

On the whole one may say that in the period of the Ghetto:

1. The Jewish group was a compact group spacially and socially. Thus we may represent this group as one "connected" region or as relatively few compact regions. These regions only rarely included foreign sections.

2. Belonging to the group was clearly marked. A yellow badge imposed from without, or a particular form of behavior (as in

dress or in speech) developed from within, made him easily recognizable by everyone. So there could be no question, either for himself or any one else, about his belonging to the Jewish group.

3. The boundary between the Jewish group and the other groups had the character of a strong and almost impassable barrier. As many facts prove, the strength of this barrier was actively maintained no less by the Jewish group than by the group outside the barrier.

4. The effect of this situation on the life of the Jewish group varied according to the sociological forces acting upon the group. The strict limitation of the space of free movement creates for a group, as for an individual, a high tension. Experimental psychology has demonstrated the tension arising in such prison-like situations. If too high a pressure from outside is applied to a group, it may result in a lack of development similar to the effect of over-pressure on the development of children. Such isolated groups under pressure are usually extremely conservative and even retarded. On the other hand, this conservatism preserves the group intact.

With this situation of the Jewish group in the Ghetto period, we may roughly compare the modern situation of the Jewish group as it existed for instance in Germany before the First World War. In prewar Germany:

1. The Jewish group could no longer be described as compact. Jews were not compelled to live in special districts. It is true that even in the modern period they were often concentrated in one part of a town. Nevertheless they were more or less distributed all over the country. Topologically, one can not represent the Jewish group at that time as one or a few connected regions, but rather as an unconnected region composed of many separated parts (Fig. XXII).

Even where Jewish individuals settled close together, the Jewish region might include foreign groups. It was no longer homogeneous. As compared with the Ghetto period (Fig. XXI), we have now to deal with a much more loose and scattered group (Fig. XXII).

We find the same result in the occupational distribution. There was in Germany some concentration of the Jews in special occupations as a result of family traditions and other factors, but some Jews were found in nearly every occupation. The topological structure of the occupational field gives the same picture of inter-mingling as the picture of the geographical field.

2. This looser connection between the parts of the group and their wider distribution involved a change of the character of the boundary between the Jewish and the other groups. This boundary was, after the "emancipation," no longer a boundary by law—

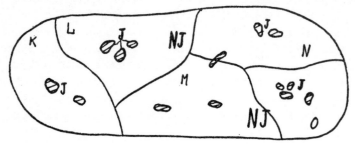

FIGURE XXII

The letters have the same significance as in Fig. XXI.

which is relatively strong, clearly defined, and easily made tangible —but a much less apparent and tangible boundary between social groups. The boundary, although still existing, lost considerably in strength and concreteness. At least for some individuals the boundary became passable.

3. Similarly the space of free movement for social action had grown greater. There indeed remained some restrictions, generally enforced from the outside, but on the whole there were many more possibilities for social activity. The pressure against the group was much weaker. As a result, there was a great deal of cultural development, and as for any emancipated group, much less conservatism. One found pronounced tendencies towards progressivism and radicalism with their concomitant advantages and disadvantages.

4. The weakening of the boundary of a group and the extension of that boundary always involves more points of contact between the group and the other groups. As a result of the closer contact, the difference in character between the groups will be somewhat lessened. The belonging of the individual to the group is no longer marked by such an obvious symbol as the yellow badge. Also the distinction of dress and habits nearly disappears.

5. With the enlarging of the space of free movement, and with the weakening of the pressure applied from without, the tension under which this group as a whole lives has doubtless decreased.

But strange as it may appear at first, this decrease of tension has brought no real relaxation to the life of the Jew, but instead has meant perhaps even higher tension in some respects. This paradoxical fact is not only a scientific problem, but one of the most disturbing elements in modern Jewish life. What this paradox means, and why it occurs, we shall best see if we now consider, not the Jewish group, but the individual Jew, and ask what forces are acting on him as an individual, and how the strength and the direction of the forces have been affected by a change in the position of his group.

If we compare the position of the individual Jew in the Ghetto period (Fig. XXIIIa) with his situation in modern times (Fig. XXIIIb), we find that he now stands much more for and by himself. With the wider spread and scattering of the Jewish group, the family or the single individual becomes functionally much more separated. Using a term of dynamic psychology, we can say that the individual, in so far as his Jewishness is concerned, becomes to a higher degree "a separated whole" than he was in the time of the Ghetto. At that time he felt the pressure to be essentially applied to the Jewish group as a whole (Fig. XXIIIa). Now as a result of the disintegration of the group, he is much more exposed to pressure as an individual. The weakening of the pressure against the Jews as a group since the Ghetto period has been accompanied by a development which has shifted the point of application of external forces from the group to the individual. So it became possible that even when the pressure on the whole group

FORCES ACTING ON THE INDIVIDUAL AND ON THE GROUP

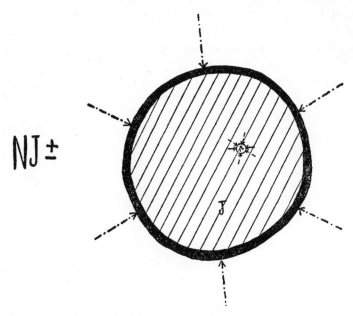

FIGURE XXIIIa.   In the Ghetto Period (corresponding to Fig. XXI)

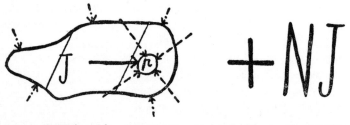

FIGURE XXIIIb.   After Emancipation (corresponding to Fig. XXII)

p, individual person
J, Jewish group
NJ, non-Jewish group
——————— force acting on the individual corresponding to his own desires.
— — — force acting on the individual applied from without.
— . — . — . force applied to the group as such.

from without was weakened, that on the individual Jew was relatively increased.

In the Ghetto period a Jew may have been exposed to especially high pressure when acting outside his group, but on the other hand there was for him some region in which he felt "at home" in which he could act freely as a member of his own group, and did not need to stand by himself against pressure from without. In other words, even when the pressure was high, there were regions in which this pressure had not the character of a differential pressure acting on the Jew as an individual person. With the intermingling of the Jewish and non-Jewish groups, the Jew has relatively more often to face as an individual the pressure against the Jews.

There is an additional factor responsible for this paradoxical effect. Like psychology, sociology will have to distinguish two kinds of forces acting on the individual: those resulting from the individual's own wishes and hopes, and those socially "induced" or applied to the individual from without by some other agent. The latter forces were greater in the Ghetto period, and led to greater pressure. On the other hand there was at that time practically no force corresponding to the individual's own wishes in the direction of the non-Jewish groups. Even if some individual had some secret wish to cross the boundary of his group, the character of this boundary as a strong and practically impassable barrier destroyed all such hopes at once. For a Jew at that period the regions outside his group probably had no very strong attraction or, to use a psychological term, had no strong "positive valence." If such a valence happened to exist, it could create only dreams, and not strong forces on the "level of reality."

In the modern period a very different situation exists for the individual. There are manifold contacts between members of the Jewish group and members of other groups. The barrier has lost its concreteness and strength. The boundary seems at least to be passable, because the difference in habits, culture, and thinking has become in many respects very small. Often there is, or at least there seems to be, almost no distance between the groups.

We know from experimental psychology of children and adults what great effect a situation in which a goal is "almost reached" has for the driving forces acting on the person. As one of many examples, we may cite the fact that prisoners who have nearly completed, for instance, three years' imprisonment, may break loose a few days before their release. Similarly, adolescents who are ready to be released in a few weeks from a reformatory not infrequently fall back on their previous bad behavior. A more detailed observation shows that in this, as in many situations in which something is almost reached, the individual is in a state of very strong conflict. This conflict arises partly from the fact that such a near-goal creates a very strong force in its direction. Furthermore, the prisoner or the adolescent about to be released feels himself already a member of the group which he is about to join. So long as he felt himself a member of the previous group he acted in accordance with the rules of that group; but now, feeling almost a member of the other group, he also feels the right and necessity of acquiring all the prerogatives of that other group.

Since the emancipation, a somewhat similar situation exists among a high percentage of Jews. As a member of a group which in many respects has fewer rights and possibilities than other groups, the individual naturally has the tendency to enter these groups as soon as his belonging to the first group is questionable. Every weakening of the boundary between his group and the other groups will increase the strength of the force in this direction. In other words, on approaching complete emancipation and therefore dissolution of the group, the individual members of the group will, in the given circumstances, be subject to an increasing conflict. The resulting behavior may be derived from this conflict-situation.

Any conflict creates tension, which leads to restlessness, unbalanced behavior, and over-emphasis in one or the other direction. Indeed the Jews are commonly characterized as being restless. The most productive type of restlessness is over-exertion in work. Some of the best work of Jewish people in the last century was partly due to this over-activity.

This restlessness is not an innate trait of the Jew, but a result of his situation. According to various observers, one of the outstanding characteristics of Jews in Palestine is the absence of this restlessness. It is especially interesting that even adults seem to change in this respect within a few months after immigration, despite the difficulties connected with adaptation to a very different country. This shows to what extent the previous behavior was due to the previous situation, a situation in which the individual was uncertain whether a disparagement of his work was attributable to its lack of merit or to the fact that its creator was a Jew. Even though the occasions for this uncertainty might have been rare, they would have the lasting effect of depriving the person of standards by which to measure the extent and limits of his ability, and in this way make him unsure of his own worth.

The conflict which leads to the restlessness of the Jews in the Diaspora centers in the individual's feelings about his belonging to the Jewish group. As a general rule, individuals who try to cross the boundary to a socially higher group face a nearly unavoidable inner conflict. Members of the socially higher groups are proud of belonging to their group and feel free to judge and act in accordance with the ideals and standards of the group. On the other hand, the person who tries to enter the higher group has to be especially careful not to show connection with the ideas of the group to which he once belonged. For this reason too his behavior is uncertain. Achad Haám has referred to this situation of emancipation as "slavery within freedom."

The conflict seems to be especially severe for young members of well-to-do families. This is in line with our statement that the strength of the conflict situation increases with the weakness of the boundary between the groups concerned: at this social level the boundary between Jewish and non-Jewish families is functionally relatively weak; on the other hand, the young person may not have had an opportunity to prove himself successful enough to become self-confident.

We have discussed the Jewish problem as an example of the situation of a minority group. One cannot, however, neglect its special nature. There are important differences between religious, national, and racial minority groups, and the strength of their tendency to assimilate varies greatly. It depends not only upon the character of the groups themselves, but also upon the character of the surrounding groups and upon the structure of the total situation.

The Jews have been regarded sometimes as a religious, sometimes as a racial group, and they themselves have been rather uncertain about the character of the group. The feeling of the average Jew of belonging to the country of his birth was in some countries (for example, in Germany) far stronger than his feeling of belonging to the Jewish group. Unlike similar minorities, the Jews have for more than a thousand years lacked a geographical region of their own, which they could regard as a "homeland." This obviously had the effect of making the unity of the group somewhat "abstract" and unreal, creating additional uncertainty for the members of the group and giving them some quality of "abnormality" in the opinion of the surrounding groups. It is not unlikely that if the establishment of a Jewish homeland in Palestine succeeds, it will affect the situation of Jews everywhere in the direction of greater normality.

We have here applied concepts of topological and vector psychology to sociological problems. This method has, among others, the advantage of permitting one to treat a sociological group as a *whole*, when such treatment is adequate; to take into account in a concrete manner the different *degrees* of unity of social groups, their different *structure* and *distribution* relative to other groups; and, finally, to pass from *group* to *individual* problems (or in the other direction) if and when it is necessary, without having to resort to a new set of concepts.

IO

WHEN FACING DANGER

(1939)

I.

THE world is suspended in balance between peace and war. Sometimes there seems to be hope that war will be averted after all; sometimes it looks as if war would start very soon. Most people hate war because it is destructive and senseless. On the other hand, those who are interested in democracy realize that there is but one of two alternatives, either to live as slaves under Fascism, or to be ready to die for democracy. Thus the heart of every freedom-loving person wavers between two opposite poles, and even more so the heart of the Jew. If the Jew is not a dreamer, he realizes what additional horrors he has to expect from both war and peace. In every European war the Jews have fought and died for their countries, and in addition have been picked out for maltreatment both by friend and enemy. I am afraid this additional Jewish plight will be worse than ever before. There is little doubt that the German Jew, who has been deprived of all means of livelihood and is now carefully excluded from the army, will nevertheless have ample chances to die for this very German "fatherland" in the next war, as he did in the last. Already, German newspapers, in other words the German government, suggest the formation of special Jewish battalions to be used in places of particularly great danger. With German machine guns in back, they will have to fight the enemy in front. The situation of the Jews in Italy and Hungary will not be much different, and certainly they will be the first to feel the scarcity of food. I am afraid that the situation of the great Jewish population of Poland, a country which at present stands on the other side of the fence, will not be much better.

But how does peace look to the Jew, a peace in which one country after the other seems to be gradually drawn into the orbit of Nazi domination or Fascist ideology? Today Nazi Germany is, doubtless, the greatest European power, having swallowed Austria, Czechoslovakia, and one might add Italy, which for all practical purposes can be considered as ruled by the German Gestapo. In all these countries, including Hungary, the outlawing of the Jews has of course been firmly established. Not less disastrous is the spreading of Nazi ideology which in times of peace is easily disseminated. Today in every country of the world not only influential Nazi agents, but also powerful groups of citizens, believe in the Fascist creed, and the greater the economic difficulties in those countries, the greater the number of adherents to this gospel. As to the Jews, Fascism necessarily means persecution and, at least, the establishment of a Ghetto. Jews have been recognized as human beings only since the ideas of the American and the French revolutions became dominant, particularly the idea of the basic equality of men. Jewish rights are inseparably bound to this philosophy of equality. A basic principle of Nazism is the inequality of men. It therefore, of necessity, denies equal rights to the Jews.

Thinking in this way of peace and war, what then should the Jew hope for? Should he hope for peace with the likelihood of the spreading of Fascism, including torture and destruction of the Jew, or should he hope for the disaster of war? The Jews are but a small atom in a turbulent world; their fate is decided by all-powerful forces, which may seem beyond the sphere of their influence. Thus the Jew might well ask himself: What shall we do? Shall we fall down and cry aloud, "Shema Yisroel," as our fathers did again and again when facing death and destruction? Little else seems to be left to the Jews in certain European countries.

But for the rest of the Jews there is still time for thought and action.

I suppose many feel as deeply as I do that action is what we need in Jewish life today. My generation in Europe has gone through four years of war, followed by years of grave economic disturbances and revolutions. It does not look as if the next ten years are going to be more quiet and comfortable. The Jewish problem will certainly be no less serious.

If it has ever been a question whether the Jewish problem is an individual or a social one, a clear-cut answer was provided by the S. A. men in the streets of Vienna who beat with steel rods any Jew irrespective of his past conduct or status. Jews all over the world now recognize that the Jewish problem is a social problem. Thus we will have to turn to sociology and social psychology, if we wish to get scientific help for its solution. Scientifically the Jewish problem has to be treated as a case of an underprivileged minority. In the Diaspora the Jew does not enjoy the same opportunities as the majority. The degree and kind of restrictions imposed upon him vary greatly in different countries and at different times. Sometimes he is practically outlawed. At other times the restrictions are merely social in nature, without much hindrance in occupational and political life. Frequently some parts of the Jewish population enjoy better conditions than parts of the non-Jewish population. By and large, however, the Jewish group as a whole has the status of an underprivileged minority.

It should be understood that any underprivileged minority is preserved as such by the more privileged majority. The emancipation of the Jews from the Ghetto has not been accomplished by Jewish action, but was brought about by a change in the needs and sentiments of the majority. Today again, it can easily be shown how any increase or decrease in the economic difficulties of the majority increases or decreases the pressure upon the Jewish minority. This is one of the reasons why Jews everywhere are necessarily interested in the welfare of the majority among whom they live.

It has been recognized long ago that the basis of anti-Semitism is partly the need of the majority for a scapegoat. Frequently in modern history it is not the majority as such but an autocratic group ruling the majority which needs the scapegoat as a means of distracting the masses. The most striking recent example is Mussolini's sudden attack on the Italian Jews against whom practically no anti-Semitic feeling had existed before. The same Mussolini, who but a few years ago was favorably disposed toward Zionism, found it wise to follow Hitler's example, or he may have been forced by Hitler to do so. Certainly nothing in the conduct of Italian Jewry has given the slightest cause for this change. Here again, the need of the majority or of their ruling élite alone has determined the fate of the Jewish community.

The Jew might as well realize that these happenings are practically independent of good or bad behavior on his part. There is nothing more erroneous than the belief of many Jews that there would be no anti-Semitism if only every Jew behaved properly. One might even say that it is the good behavior of the Jews, their hard work, their efficiency and success as business men, physicians, and lawyers, which give momentum to the anti-Semitic drive. Anti-Semitism cannot be stopped by the good behavior of the individual Jew, because it is not an individual, but a social problem.

How little relation exists between Jewish conduct and anti-Semitism is well illustrated by the way the majority shifts its official reasons for maltreatment. For hundreds of years the Jews have been persecuted for religious reasons. Today racial theories serve as pretext. The reasons are easily changed according to whatever seems to be the most efficient argument at the moment. I have been told that in this country one of the most influential associations of manufacturers is working with two types of pamphlets. One of these pamphlets, used when a group of workers or middle-class people are approached, pictures the Jew as a capitalist and as an international banker. But if the same propagandist speaks to an audience of manufacturers, he uses a pamphlet which pictures the Jews as communists.

The Jew answering accusations should realize that they are but a surface, below which deeper social problems are hidden even in those cases when the argument is put forth in good faith. The need of the majority for a scapegoat grows out of tension, e.g. from an economic depression. Scientific experiments prove that this need is particularly strong in tensions which are due to an autocratic regime. No "logical" argument will destroy these basic forces. One cannot hope to combat Father Coughlin efficiently by telling everybody how good the Jews are.

More than words of self-defense are necessary to change social reality. Certainly Jews will have to try everything to ally themselves with any other force seriously fighting Fascism. Being but few in number it is incumbent upon us to try to win the help of other groups. However, the Jew will have to realize that for him as well as for any other underprivileged group the following statement holds: Only the efforts of the group itself will achieve the emancipation of the group.

There is one field of action left to the Jew, where the results depend mainly upon himself. This is the field of Jewish life.

II.

What makes the Jews a group and what makes an individual a member of the Jewish group? I know that many Jews are deeply concerned and puzzled by this problem. They have no clear answer and their whole life is in danger of becoming meaningless, as it has become meaningless for thousands of German half-Jews and quarter-Jews who must face fate without knowing why. Historically this problem is relatively new to the Jew. There has been a time, only one hundred and fifty years ago, when even in Germany belonging to the Jewish group was an accepted and unquestioned fact. During the time of the Ghetto Jews might have been under pressure as a group; the individual Jew, however, had a social unit to which he clearly belonged. The Jews in Poland, Lithuania and other Eastern European countries have maintained what might be termed a national life which gave to the individual a "social home." When coming to America, the Eastern Jews brought much of this group life with them. They have kept alive the inner cohesive forces of the group.

It is well to realize that every underprivileged minority group is kept together not only by cohesive forces among its members but also by the boundary which the majority erects against the crossing of an individual from the minority to the majority group. It is in the interest of the majority to keep the minority in its underprivileged status. There are minorities which are kept together almost entirely by such a wall around them. The members of these minorities show certain typical characteristics resulting from this situation. Every individual likes to gain in social status. Therefore the member of an underprivileged group will try to leave it for the more privileged majority. In other words, he will try to do what in the case of Negroes is called "passing," in the case of Jews, "assimilation." It would be an easy solution of the minority problem if it could be done away with through individual assimilation. Actually, however, such a solution is impossible for any underprivileged group. Equal rights for women could not be attained by one after the other being granted the right to vote; the Negro problem cannot be solved by individual "passing." A few Jews might be fully accepted by non-Jews. This chance, however, is today more meager than ever and certainly it is absurd to believe that fifteen million Jews can sneak over the boundary one by one.

What then is the situation of a member of a minority group kept together merely by the repulsion of the majority? The basic factor in his life is his wish to cross this insuperable boundary. Therefore, he lives almost perpetually in a state of conflict and tension. He dislikes or even hates his own group because it is nothing but a burden to him. Like an adolescent who does not wish to be a child any longer but who knows that he is not accepted as an adult, such a person stands at the border-line of his group, being neither here nor there. He is unhappy and shows the typical characteristics of a marginal man who does not know where he belongs. A Jew of this type will dislike everything specifically Jewish, for he will see in it that which keeps him away from the majority for which he is longing. He will show dislike for those Jews who are outspokenly so and will frequently indulge in self-hatred.

There is one more characteristic peculiar to minority groups kept together merely by outside pressure as contrasted with the members of a minority who have a positive attitude towards their own group The latter group will have an organic life of its own. It will show organization and inner strength. A minority kept together only from outside is in itself chaotic. It is composed of a mass of individuals without inner relations with each other, a group unorganized and weak.

Historically, the Jews living in the Diaspora were kept together partly by the inner cohesive forces of the group and partly by the pressure of hostile majorities. The importance of these two factors has varied at different times and in different countries. In some parts of Eastern Europe the positive attitude has been strengthened by cultural superiority to the environment. In this country the positive attitude is also strong as yet. We should not, however, be blind to the fact that for quite a number of Jews "being forced together" has become the dominant, or at least an important, aspect of their inner relation to Judaism.

I have heard Jewish students in the Middle West say that they feel more like non-Jewish Midwesterners than like Jews from New York. Since the religious issue has lost importance for Jews and Gentiles alike, there does not exist an easily tangible difference between both groups. To preach Jewish religion or nationalism to such Jews is not likely to have any deep effect. To speak about the glorious history and culture of the Jewish people will not convince them either. They would not want to sacrifice their lives and happiness to things past. In places with a limited Jewish population, and particularly among the adolescents, one finds many who are utterly bewildered about why and in what respect they belong to the Jewish group. One might be able to help some of them by explaining that it is not similarity or dissimilarity of individuals that constitutes a group, but interdependence of fate. Any normal group, and certainly any developed and organized one contains and should contain individuals of very different character. Two members of one family might be less alike than two members of different families; but in spite of differences in character and interest, two individuals will belong to the same group if their fates are interdependent. Similarly in spite of divergent opinions about religious or political ideas, two persons might still belong to the same group.

It is easy enough to see that the common fate of all Jews makes them a group in reality. One who has grasped this simple idea will not feel that he has to break away from Judaism altogether whenever he changes his attitude toward a fundamental Jewish issue, and he will become more tolerant of differences of opinion among Jews. What is more, a person who has learned to see how much his own fate depends upon the fate of his entire group will be ready and even eager to take over a fair share of responsibility for its welfare. This realistic understanding of the sociological facts is very important for establishing a firm social ground, especially for those who have not grown up in a Jewish environment.

III.

I have already mentioned that problems of an underprivileged minority are directly related to the conditions of the majority. Anxious to retain a friendly attitude on the part of the majority, important sections of Jewry try to avoid aggressiveness and tend to hush up disagreeable events. The motive behind this policy is partly—but only partly—correct. Jews should clearly distinguish two situations, one dealing with friends and neutrals and the other dealing with enemies. It is a clear symptom of maladjustment for a person to relate everything to Jewish questions and to bring up the Jewish problem in every situation. But to keep quiet in regard to Jewish questions where it would be natural to discuss them is no less a sign of maladjustment. Experience shows that on the whole, non-Jews are less sensitive to an overemphasis of one's Jewishness than to the tendency of aping things non-Jewish. A member of a minority who emphasizes his belonging to it obviously does not try to sneak over the borderline, and therefore does not need to be rejected. Those members of the minority, however, whose conduct seems to imply an effort to "pass," will provoke immediate counteraction.

Loyalty to the Jewish group therefore furthers rather than hinders friendly relations with non-Jews. Both natural relations between human beings and the political interest of the Jews demand the establishment of friendly bonds with as many groups and individuals of the majority as possible.

However, the Jews should also be clear about those situations in which friendly approaches are out of place. Friendliness is no appropriate response to an aggressor. In recent years we have seen in world politics how undignified, morally distasteful and unwise is the policy of appeasing an aggressor. It is both shameful and stupid to talk to a man who is determined to destroy you. For the enemy such friendly talk means only that you are either too weak or too cowardly to fight him. We should not be mistaken about the following point either: the onlooker, who is not yet prejudiced, might be won over and brought to sympathize with an individual or a group of people who fight back with all their power against an aggressor, while he will show very little sympathy for people who bow to an insult. Britain has felt the truth of this simple observation rather keenly within the last two years.

I hope that Jews in America will recognize this truth before it is too late. There are now many among us who adopt the attitude of "talking things over" and "getting together" without the necessary discrimination. This attitude is entirely correct and advisable with friends and neutrals, but not if we have to deal with groups which have made up their mind to destroy us.

The Jew will have to realize, and he will have to realize it fast, that in fighting Nazis and their allies it does not pay to be polite. There is only one way to fight an enemy, and this is to return blow for blow, to strike back immediately, and if possible, harder. Jews can expect to get active help from others only if they themselves show that they have the courage and the determination to stand up for a fight of self-defense. Jews will have to adapt themselves to a new scale of risks in their daily actions. The situation of world Jewry seems to leave only one choice open: the choice between living like the Jews in Germany, Austria, Czechoslovakia, which means living as slaves, doomed to starvation and suicide, or being ready to fight with all means required and, if necessary, to die in this fight for freedom and against extermination.

This choice is not a pleasant one, and it may seem particularly depressing to young people. But the young will understand that it is more honest, more dignified and more in line with the spirit of both Judaism and Americanism, to react promptly and vigorously against the first insult than to wait until the enemy has grown strong enough to impose his will by force. To overlook insult may seem generous to the sophisticated mind. But in a situation like ours, where the very existence of the Jewish people is at stake, we cannot afford the luxury of this gesture. Aside from the moral issue, a man who does not show backbone acts unwisely. He invites the bestiality of the mob which is always ready to have its brutal fun but is afraid to stick out its neck when it knows that it will be resisted.

Such a fight in self-defense would be more than a self-centered act. It would have a direct bearing upon the struggle of the majority for the solution of their economic and political problems. We have emphasized that the fate of the Jews is bound up with the economic welfare of the majority. Unfortunately, it will be impossible to solve the economic problem so long as underprivileged minorities can provide cheap labor and political scapegoats. As matters stand today, the Jews as a group can hardly do anything more for the economic welfare of the country than to prevent the forces of Fascism from using the suppression of the Jews as a steppingstone towards the suppression of other racial and religious groups and the masses of the people in general.

It would be a mistake to believe that the man who has made up his mind to be ready for any action and danger which fate might hold in store for him lives in a continuous stage of tension, anxiety and stress. The opposite is true. Anxiety is characteristic of one who is confused and does not know what to do. One who faces danger rather than waits to be crushed under the enemy's heel can again live in a clear atmosphere and is able to enjoy life even when surrounded by danger.

I I

BRINGING UP THE JEWISH CHILD

(1940)

AS THE number of free countries keeps dwindling, the attitudes and actions of the coming generation of Jews in the United States will be of the utmost importance for the Jewish people as a whole, in Europe and Palestine as well as in America. To a large degree, the actions will be determined by the attitudes which the growing children acquire. Therefore a realistic understanding by Jewish parents and teachers of the psychological and pedagogical problems involved is of the highest importance. We shall endeavor to clarify these problems by discussing the social setting which confronts the child. Only an education which takes stock of this setting can hope to be successful.

I.

Let us consider a town of medium size in the Middle West containing a small Jewish group living in good relations with the Gentiles. The Jews, mainly middle-class people, while taking care of their own charity problems, co-operate fully in the economic, political and social enterprises of the town. And it might even happen that a number of Gentiles contribute to Jewish charities.

There would not at first be many occasions where the non-Jewish environment makes the growing Jewish child feel he is classified as different from Gentile children. He might go through nursery school and kindergarten up to the fourth grade of elementary school before his first experience of being called "dirty Jew," perhaps on the occasion of a children's fight.

But when the growing child approaches the age where parent: are accustomed to consider friendships between boys and girls as possibly leading to marriage, he is likely not to receive invitations to Gentile families for social occasions. However, the line is not always clearly and sharply defined; often it is doubtful whether the restriction is due to the child's being a Jew or to some other reason. It might happen that not until he attempts to secure employment does the young Jew personally encounter any severe restrictions.

But the Jewish boy or girl desiring to enter a university comes up against a definite classification. It is no secret that in most of the important universities an unofficial but nevertheless definite quota limits the number of Jews, particularly in professional schools. Only Jewish fraternities and sororities are open to Jewish students. Thus, his classification as a Jew receives an emphasis which often enough surpasses considerably the desires of the student.

How do the Jewish students react to this situation? There are any number who are quite able "to take it." That is, they show a well adapted and balanced behavior, living happily and mingling with both Jewish and non-Jewish groups.

There are, however, a large number of Jewish students who show decided lack of adjustment. To one who has come to America from pre-Hitler Germany it is quite impressive to find such typical signs of Jewish maladjustment as over-tension, loudness, over-aggressiveness, excessively hard work—sometimes to an even higher degree here than over there.

II.

What, then, are the factors that determine whether the individual Jew will show a balanced or an unbalanced behavior, and what should education do to secure balanced behavior?

One might be tempted to argue in this way: anti-Semitism is only one of many difficulties the child is going to encounter. There are the ordinary difficulties in school, difficulties with his parents and relatives, difficulties with his friends. As a matter of fact, the occasions when a child is likely to meet with anti-Semitism, under the circumstances described, are rare compared with the frequency of the other problems. If, then, one looks upon the difficulties arising from anti-Semitism not from the point of view of the Jews as a group but from that of the single individual, could one not argue, even with some show of realism, that there need be no specific preparation of the child to meet anti-Semitism? Should it not suffice to strengthen the child's general ability to cope with difficulties, particularly his ability to take social setbacks? At least in early childhood, it could be argued, there seems to be no necessity for any specific preparation. It should be sufficient to help the child if and when the actual problems arise.

There are factors which favor such an attitude on the part of Jewish parents. It is always unpleasant to weigh down a young child with additional problems. To make the child Jew-conscious is likely to make him feel different from his non-Jewish school-chums and playmates; it raises questions in him and may lead to some separation. Is it not better, then, to soft-pedal this problem as long as possible, until the child will be strong enough to "take it"? Should that not be the proper pedagogical policy, at least in all cases where the general environment is sufficiently friendly to exempt the young child from anti-Semitic difficulties?

There is a second feeling often underlying such an attitude among parents. It was typical of a large sector of the Jewish population in pre-Hitler Germany. The projection of the Jewish problem on occasions where there was no absolute necessity was considered dangerous for the Jewish position, as likely to increase the separation of Jews and non-Jews. It was hoped that by, so to speak, de-emphasizing this problem as long as possible and in as many situations as possible the whole Jewish problem would gradually disappear.

It is my belief that such a procedure does not help the child but, on the contrary, is most likely to have the opposite effect. It is a poor pedagogical policy, likely to bring the child into unneces-

sarily grave conflicts; it weakens his ability to cope with the difficulties; besides, his behavior is likely not to decrease but to incease
anti-Semitism.

To see this clearly we shall have to discuss in some detail the
nature of the psychological problems involved from the point of
view of the growing child himself.

III.

The underlying problem is not by any means exclusively a
Jewish one. A member of any less privileged group has to face it.
This holds true to an astonishingly high degree not only in those
cases where the lack of privilege comes from social discrimination,
as, for example, against Negroes in the United States, but also
where it arises from bodily defects, such as deafness. Basic for the
general problem is the question: What does belongingness to a
group mean to an individual, and how does that affect his behavior
in certain situations? I would like to make this point clear by
citing two non-Jewish examples.

A young Negress in one of the Northern industrial centers who
is engaged in housework is encouraged by her white teacher to take
the civil service examination. She passes at the top of the list and
is assigned to a public swimming-pool. Negro patronage of this
swimming-pool has been prohibited; nor does the director wish
to employ Negroes. His objections are overruled by the civil service
authorities. He employs the Negro girl in a lower capacity than
she merits—in cleaning work. The girl works without complaint.
After a few weeks she thinks of swimming in the pool herself.
Immediately a group of white boys approach her, treat her none
too gently, make her stop swimming. The shock is so great that she
not only quits her job but refuses to try for any other job to which
she is eligible in the civil service. The white teacher from whom
I got these facts told me that she came upon the Negress some
time later as an elevator girl in a department store. The teacher
tried to encourage her to apply once more for a civil service position, but the girl seemed to have lost all faith and all interest in
anything better than a subservient place.

Such a degree of breakdown made me suspect that as a child

this Negress had had particularly friendly relations with white children on an equal footing. An inquiry showed that she had indeed grown up in a group of children without discrimination between whites and Negroes.

The fundamental problem is revealed even more clearly when we consider certain cases which at first glance seem to have very little connection with minority problems.

The histories of foster-children frequently reveal rather tragic developments. A child adopted very young grows up believing his foster-parents to be his true parents. They do not tell the child the truth, wishing him to regard them as his true parents. It is not unusual, however, that around the age of fifteen or seventeen he is told by someone that he is "merely" a foster-child. The result is frequently devastating beyond all expectation. There are cases where the child who was a good student at school loses his high rank, stops taking any work seriously and turns into a vagabond. Such reactions have been observed where the foster-parents continue to give the child every proof of their undiminishing love and loyalty, and nothing has changed in the "objective" relations of the family. In such cases the deplorable effect seems to be excessively out of proportion, for nothing else than the child's feeling of belongingness to his foster-parents has been changed.

These experiences have induced authorities in charge of the placement of children to advise the foster-parents to inform the children at a very early age about their true situation. The foster-child is usually told that most children are given to their parents without their choice. He, however, has been *chosen* by his parents from a whole lot of children and thus can be particularly proud to be a "chosen child." The result often is that the foster-child actually brags that he is a chosen child. In adolescence he has no difficulties in facing problems which might have shaken the very foundation of his existence had he learned the truth only then.

IV.

Why does it make so much difference whether the foster-child learns about his true situation at three years of age or at fifteen?

The answer, at least a partial one, can be found in the following fact. The group to which an individual belongs is the ground on which he stands, which gives or denies him social status, gives or denies him security and help. The firmness or weakness of this ground might not be consciously perceived, just as the firmness of the physical ground on which we tread is not always thought of. Dynamically, however, the firmness and clearness of this ground determine what the individual wishes to do, what he can do, and how he will do it. This is true equally of the social ground as of the physical.

The development of experimental psychology shows more and more definitely that a person and what might be called his psychological environment cannot be treated as separate entities but are dynamically one field. For instance, recently experiments have shown that the intelligence of a child is greatly changed by different types of surroundings. There is plenty of evidence that stability or instability of the surroundings makes for stability or instability of the growing child. It is well known how the mood or tension of the mother will affect the child's mood or tension.

The same fact can be stated in another, if more technical, way by saying that the growth of a child to a differentiated and stable person is functionally identical with, or at least very closely related to, the development of a differentiated and stable psychological surrounding of the child. Seen with the eyes of the child, his world is at first undifferentiated, and only a few areas, such as the experiences of feeding, acquire definite form and color. Gradually the well-defined parts of his world become more extensive. One says "the child learns, acquires knowledge, orients himself." One should realize, however, that this learning means something more: the very building up of the world in which the child lives, of the ground on which he stands. From early childhood, social facts, particularly the feeling of belongingness to certain groups, are among the most fundamental constituents of this growing world, and determine what the individual considers right or wrong, his wishes and his goals.

The behavior of our Negress can now be better understood. She grew up among both Negro and white friends who treated each other on an equal basis. She believed literally in the equal rights which, as she learned at school, are granted by the American constitution to every citizen. In short, she grew up with the ideology of equality of Negro and white, and her outlook for the future was based on this ideology. It is understandable that the world of such a girl must be rocked to its depths the moment this belief proves to be an illusion.

It does not matter very much whether the girl was treated more or less severely in the swimming-pool. What matters is the *meaning* this action had for her change of feeling about the inter-relation between the group to which she belonged and the other groups. The girl found the social structure in her psychological world, which had been slowly built up for years, suddenly shattered. Now she was disoriented. She lost the basis for directed actions, for she no longer knew whether an action which she had hitherto believed to be an approach to a certain goal really had that direction. Moreover, her faith in the stability of the world was severely broken down, and without such stability it is meaningless to make plans ahead.

Similar causes are behind the despair of the foster-child despite the fact that "objectively" nothing has changed. His own position in regard to group-belonging has changed, and therefore a change of relation to the totality of facts existing in his world has taken place. He too has seen a world built up for years break down in a moment; and his faith in the stability of the ground on which he stands, and hence his willingness to make plans for the future, is lost.

Two deductions for the Jewish problem are easily made:

(1) In judging the importance of experiences related to our belonging to, or our status in, a social group, or related to any other constitutents of the ground on which we stand, one should not give much weight to the frequency or the unpleasantness of those experiences themselves. Instead one should consider the meaning of those experiences in terms of how much the structure of the life-space of the individual is changed. Jewish parents, then, should learn to realize that it does not much matter how often the child

will experience prejudices or whether he will experience them in a rough or polite manner. What is important is the significance of these experiences in determining the position of the Jewish group to the non-Jewish group, and also in determining the sphere of situations in which belonging to the Jewish group is considered a major factor.

(2) It is of first importance that a stable social ground be laid very early. The same experience of being called "foster-child" which might upset the fifteen-year-old boy who was not aware of the real situation will have little or no effect at all on the child who was properly introduced to his real situation at the age of three. The variety of social structures to which a growing child can adapt himself in a relatively stable way is astonishingly great. It seems, however, extremely difficult to establish a new stable social ground after one has broken down.

V.

The group a person belongs to serves not only as a source of help and protection; it also implies certain regulations and taboos. In other words, it narrows the individual's "space of free movement." This is very important for the question of adaptation of the individual to the group. The basic problem can be stated thus: Can the individual satisfy his own personal needs to a sufficient degree without interfering unduly with the life and purpose of the group?

If belonging to a certain group hinders rather than helps the individual in achieving his dominant goals, a conflict between him and the group arises, even an eagerness to leave the group. The well known anti-Semitism of some Jews is an expression of the individual Jew's dislike of belongingness to the Jewish group. In Germany that was clearly visible in the relation of the German Jews to the Eastern Jews; in the United States in the relation of the Jews of Spanish origin to the Jews of German origin, or more recently of the Jews of German to the Jews of Polish or Russian origin. The same trends exist, clearly enough, between richer and poorer Jewish fraternities on the college campus.

There also seems to exist in every underprivileged group a tendency to accept the values of the more privileged group in a given society. The member of the underprivileged group therefore becomes excessively sensitive to everything within his own group that does not conform to those values, because it makes him feel that he belongs to a group whose standards are lower. Such feeling against one's own group conflicts with the natural tendency of the

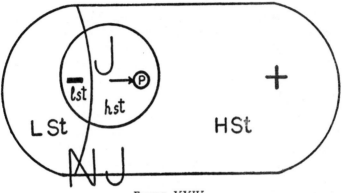

FIGURE *XXIV*

J, Jewish group; *NJ*, non-Jewish group; *LSt* and *HSt*, lower and higher social strata of non-Jews; *lst* and *hst*, lower and higher social strata of Jews; *P*, person; →, force acting on the individual in the direction away from *lst*

The dislike which the member (*P*) of an underprivileged minority (*J*) shows against those sections of his group (*lst*) which are dissimilar to the higher social strata (*HSt*) of the majority (*NJ*) is increased by the feeling that the existence of those sections involves the danger that the minority as a whole will be regarded by the majority as a part of the lower strata.

individual in favor of it. The result is a typically ambivalent attitude on the part of members of an underprivileged group toward their own group.

VI.

The breakdown of the foster-child has its parallel in the fact that the most severe breakdowns resulting from Nazi anti-Semitism have occurred among half- or quarter-Jews who had believed themselves to be good Catholics or Protestants. These unhappy people experienced a collapse of their social ground when the right of belongingness to the group of which they had felt a part all their years was suddenly denied them. Only to a lesser degree, the foundations upon which the Jews have been living all over the world were shaken when Germany, a country considered one of the most enlightened and best educated, resorted to violent Jewish persecution. This was a blow to the favored ideology of many Jews that anti-Semitism should be regarded as a "prejudice" which "well-educated people do not have" and which one can hope to overcome with "enlightenment." It made obvious the fact that this problem cannot be treated on an individual, private basis; it has to be recognized as a social problem of groups.

For the lack of adjustment observable among many Jewish individuals in the United States, another factor might, however, be more important. This is the position of many Jews as "marginal men."

Recently an eastern college co-ed, keen, beautiful, successful, and therefore on the whole in a particularly desirable position, expressed this feeling as follows:

You may have noticed that I am the middle speaker. It's a very appropriate place for me, I think, not because I strike a mean between them, but rather because I am on the fence. I haven't quite made up my mind as to what I think or why I think it. And in that, I am typical of the Jewish people.

Look at me. I'm neither here nor there. As a Jewess, I don't amount to much. I come to services when I have to; I've been told that mine is a precious heritage, but I haven't the slightest idea what it is. I can name quite a number of relatively unimportant English poets—but do I know who is the greatest Jewish poet? No. My education has been exclusively Christian. My virtues are the Christian virtues—at least my conceptions are. Occasionally, I discover something in me that is characteristically Jewish—and I am surprised, almost estranged from myself. I know I'm Jewish because I've been told so, because I have Jewish friends. Aside from that, it doesn't mean very much to me.

So you see, as a Jewess I don't amount to much. But I'm not much better as an American either. Here at school I move in a charmed circle of Jews. The other circle, the non-Jews, are oblivious of me, and I of them. Occasionally, the circles touch, sometimes more, sometimes less. I become friendly with some one in the other circle. But self-consciously friendly. If it's a boy, I wonder just how he thinks of me; he wonders what his fraternity brothers are saying. If it's a girl, we both congratulate ourselves mentally on our overstepping the bonds of racial prejudice. When I read the Phi Beta Kappa list, I'm careful to point out how many of the chosen people are Jewish. I'm always conscious that I am Jewish whether I hide it or try to impress it upon others.

So what am I? According to Jews, I'm American. According to Americans, I'm Jewish. And I'm wrong, utterly wrong; in being that way. And so it is only by pushing people like me off the fence—which side isn't so important, so long as it's off the fence—that Jews are ever going to be freed from anti-Semitism. We must remove the beam from our own eyes.

This uncertainty, which is rather typical of many young Jews, can hardly be due to the fact that the Jewish individual is not only a Jew but an American too. Brandeis's famed statement, in which he urged that double loyalty does not lead to ambiguity, is sociologically sound. That is particularly clear in the United States, which includes so many minority groups of more or less national character, such as the Irish, the Poles, the Germans, the Swedes. Furthermore, every individual belongs to many overlapping groups: to his family, his friends, his professional or business group, and so on. (See Fig. XX, page 147.) He can be loyal to all of them without being thrown into a constant state of conflict and uncertainty.

Not the *belonging to many groups* is the cause of the difficulty, but an *uncertainty* of belongingness.

In practically every underprivileged group a number of people will be found who, although regarded by the privileged majority as not belonging to them, feel themselves not really belonging to the underprivileged minority. Frequently it is the more privileged people within the underprivileged group, or those people whose open or secret intent it is to pass the line, who are in the position of what the sociologists call "marginal men." They are people who belong neither here nor there, standing "between" the groups. The psychological difficulties which the marginal man has to face—his uncertainty, his instability, and often self-hate, due to the more or less permanent state of conflict in which he finds himself—are well known to the student of sociology.

The frequency of "marginal" persons in an underprivileged group is likely to increase the more the differences between the privileged and underprivileged groups decrease, with the resulting paradox that the betterment of the group might increase the uncertainty and tension of the individual.

For the modern Jew there exists an additional factor to increase his uncertainty. He is frequently uncertain about the way he belongs to the Jewish group, and to what degree. Especially since religion has become a less important social matter, it is rather difficult to describe positively the character of the Jewish group as a whole. A religious group with many atheists? A Jewish race with a great diversity of racial qualities among its members? A nation without a state or a territory of its own containing the majority of its people? A group combined by one culture and tradition but actually having in most respects the different values and ideals of the nations in which it lives? There are, I think, few chores more bewildering than that of determining positively the character of the Jewish group. It is not easy to see why such a group should be preserved as a separate unit, why it has not entirely given up its will to live, and why the nations have refused to grant the Jews full assimilation.

No wonder many Jews are uncertain about what it means to belong to the Jewish group, and whether as individuals they should identify themselves with it or should try to break away. No wonder that frequently a Jew may shift his attitude as to what the Jewish group means to him; and if he has lost faith in religion, or has lost belief in what he used to consider the special ideals or mission of the Jews, he is likely to show a strong tendency to break loose from the group altogether.

The position of staying on the boundary between two groups ("on the fence"), of being in both groups but really in neither, might be natural for the biological half-Jews. We should realize, however, that a similar and not less difficult situation exists for those who might be called "social half-Jews," those who are not fully decided about their belongingness to the Jews. Those marginal men and women are in somewhat the same position as an adolescent who is no longer a child and certainly does not want to be a child any longer, but who knows at the same time that he is not really accepted as a grown-up. This uncertainty about the ground on which he stands and the group to which he belongs often makes the adolescent loud, restless, at once timid and aggressive, over-sensitive and tending to go to extremes, over-critical of others and himself.

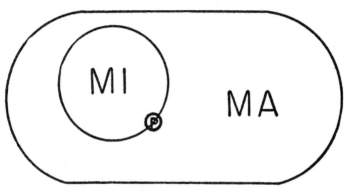

Figure XXV

The mariginal man. The person (*P*) standing on the boundary between the minority group *MI* and the majority group *MA*.

The marginal Jew is condemned for his lifetime to remain in a similar situation. Wherever Jewish questions come up he sees with the eyes of both the Jew and the non-Jew. That would be entirely in order if he were clear about the issue and if he knew clearly what his personal values were, because then he would stand on firm ground for making reasonable and fair decisions. The marginal Jew, however, does not as a rule feel sufficiently rooted in either of these groups to be clear and confident about his views and about his personal relations to either side. He is therefore compelled to remain in a rather vague and uncertain but permanent inner conflict. He is the "eternal adolescent." He shows the same unhappiness and lack of adjustment.

VII.

History amply shows that "good behavior" on the part of the Jew is by no means an insurance against anti-Semitism. On the whole, the forces acting against the Jews are mainly due to circumstances within the non-Jewish majority, for instance, situations which call for a scapegoat. These forces are to a high degree independent of Jewish conduct. However, as far as the behavior of the Jewish group is relevant, it might well be argued that in the long run more serious trouble develops from their superior than from their inferior performance. In Germany it was the economic, social, and cultural achievement of the Jews that gave momentum to the anti-Semitism. If there were any sense in the attempt to regulate the qualities of Jews, one would have to prescribe this: To avoid anti-Semitism, don't train Jewish youth in superior qualities; make them all average or, even better, below average!

Not altogether happy, either, is the effect which the soft-pedaling and, so to speak, privatizing of the Jewish problem has on the amount of anti-Semitism that the individual Jew is likely to encounter. One might classify Jews into three groups: those who over-emphasize their Jewishness, those who behave normally, and those who try to hide or to under-emphasize their Jewishness. The individual in the middle group who knows in what situation and to what degree to emphasize his Jewishness probably fares best of all. As for the others, the Gentile is more likely to react without hostility to those who over-emphasize than to those who hide their Jewishness. So long as the Gentile does not want a full assimilation, it is evident that he will become easily suspicious against the third type, but feel rather safe in relation to the first. For the uncertain behavior of individuals in the third group would seem to make it more hazardous to give equal privileges to them than to individuals whose position and probable actions are quite clear:

the latter are less likely to use equal status in professional life, business or politics, for the purpose of trying to cross the line in a field where such crossing is not wanted.

We may conclude, then, that in regard to the Jewish problem the action of Jewish parents should be the same as in matters of sex or any other education, namely, *true, open, and realistic.* These are the considerations to act on:

(1) The basic fact is that their child is going to be a member of a less privileged minority group, and he will have to face this fact.

(2) The attempt to keep this problem away from the child as long as possible, and softpedal it, will in all likelihood make for greater difficulties in adjustment later on.

(3) This applies just as much in a community where the child is so fortunate as not to encounter anti-Semitic difficulties in his early life; parents should realize that the problem is bound to arise at some time, and the sooner it is faced, the better.

(4) Such an early build-up of a clear and positive feeling of belongingness to the Jewish group is one of the few effective things that Jewish parents can do for the later happiness of their children. In this way parents can minimize the ambiguity and the tension inherent in the situation of the Jewish minority group, and thus counteract various forms of maladjustment resulting therefrom.

(5) Outstanding among the techniques that parents should employ is the treatment of Jewish problems not as an individual and private matter but as a social issue. For instance, to press the child harder for good behavior, or to raise his personal ambition higher than is customary in the Gentile majority, puts the child merely in a state of keener tension that makes for less easy adaptation. Parents should from the very beginning stress the social aspect of the situation. This is more realistic and helps to prevent the personal uncertainty and self-accusation or self-pity which otherwise are the likely results of anti-Semitic experiences.

(6) A better understanding of the sociological problems involved is of particular value to the Jewish adolescent. For it can help him to solve one of the most bewildering puzzles, mentioned previously—what kind of a group the Jews are, whether he personally belongs to them. He will often feel himself more like some Gentile friends than like some Jews, and he is apt to make this feeling of similarity or dissimilarity his measuring-stick for group-belongingness. It is true that some sociologists have made one or another kind of similarity between members the defining mark of a group. However, similarity between persons merely permits their classification, their subsumption under the same abstract concept, whereas belonging to the same social group means concrete, dynamic interrelation between persons. A husband, a wife, and a baby are less similar to each other, in spite of their being a strong natural group, than the baby is to other babies, or the husband to other men, or the wife to other women. Strong and well-organized groups, far from being fully homogeneous, are bound to contain a variety of different sub-groups and individuals. It is not similarity or dissimilarity that decides whether two individuals belong to the same or to different groups, but *social interaction or other types of interdependence*. A group is best defined as *a dynamic whole based on interdependence rather than on similarity*.

As a rule, the adolescent is well able to understand this fact. It will help him to see that his belonging or not belonging to the Jewish group is not a matter mainly of similarity or dissimilarity, nor even one of like or dislike. He will understand that regardless of whether the Jewish group is a racial, religious, national, or cultural one, the fact that it is classified by the majority as a distinct group is what counts. He will be ready to accept the variety of opinions and beliefs or other dissimilarities within the Jewish group as something quite as natural as in any other group. He will see that the main criterion of belongingness is *interdependence of fate*. Young American Jews may abhor Jewish national mysticism; they may not be willing to suffer for cultural or religious values which they do not fully understand, or perhaps even dislike; but they must be sufficiently fact-minded to see clearly their interdependence of fate with the rest of the American Jews and indeed with the Jews all over the world.

The feeling of belongingness based on such a realistic sociological understanding of interdependence would, I think, go a long way toward a proper balance in Jewish action. It should prevent the individual from over-emphasizing the Jewish problem, but at the same time create a willingness to accept a fair amount of responsibility for his own group. It should help to clear away the fog of uncertainty and conflicting feelings, which are paralyzing the action of so many of us today.

(7) Parents should not be afraid of so-called "double allegiance." Belonging to more than one overlapping group is natural and necessary for everyone. The real danger lies in standing "nowhere"—in being a "marginal man," an "eternal adolescent."

I2

SELF-HATRED AMONG JEWS

(1941)

THAT self-hatred is present among Jews is a fact that the non-Jew would hardly believe, but which is well known among the Jews themselves. It is a phenomenon which has been observed ever since the emancipation of the Jews. Professor Lessing treated this topic in Germany (1930) in a book, *Der Jüdische Selbsthass* ("Jewish Self-Hate"). Novels like that of Ludwig Lewisohn (*Island Within*, 1928), which pictures the New York Jew around 1930, and those of Schnitzler, who deals with the problems of the Austrian Jew in the period around 1900, are striking in the similarity of the problems which they show to exist. In these different countries, the same conflicts arise and Jews of the various social strata and professions attempt the same variety of solutions.

Jewish self-hatred is both a group phenomenon and an individual phenomenon. In Europe, outstanding examples of a hostile sentiment in one Jewish group against another were those of the German or Austrian Jew against the East European Jew, and, more recently, the attitude of the French Jew toward the German Jew. That all the troubles the Jews had in Germany were due to the bad conduct of the East European Jew was an opinion not infrequently heard among German Jews. In this country, the resentment of the Spanish Jew against the immigrating German Jew, and the hostility of the latter to the East European Jew form a parallel to the European situation.

Speaking in terms of individuals rather than groups, the self-hatred of a Jew may be directed against the Jews as a group, against a particular fraction of the Jews, against his own family, or against himself. It may be directed against Jewish institutions, Jewish mannerisms, Jewish language, or Jewish ideals.

There is an almost endless variety of forms which Jewish self-hatred may take. Most of them, and the most dangerous forms, are a kind of indirect, under-cover self-hatred. If I should count the instances where I have encountered open and straightforward contempt among Jews, I could name but a few. The most striking, for me, was the behavior of a well-educated Jewish refugee from Austria on the occasion of his meeting a couple of other Jewish refugees. In a tone of violent hatred, he burst out into a defense of Hitler on the ground of the undesirable characteristics of the German Jew.

But these are rare incidents. In most cases, expression of hatred of the Jew against his fellow Jew or against himself as a Jew is more subtle. This hatred is so blended with other motives that it is difficult to decide in any one particular case whether or not self-hatred is involved. Take the well-educated Jewish atheist who finally consented to deliver an address at a temple. During the service which preceded his talk, he told me about the pain he experiences on seeing a *talith* (prayer shawl), and how this aversion was first implanted in him by his father's negative attitude toward the synagogue. Have we to deal here with a form of anti-Jewish sentiment or just the great aversion of the atheist for religion? Does the rich Jewish merchant who refuses to contribute anything to a Jewish charity hate his own people or is he just miserly? The Jewish head of a department or a store may seem to lean over backward not to employ Jews; but perhaps what he does is actually the maximum that can be done under the circumstances.

It occurs infrequently—although it does happen once in a while —that a Jewish person frankly admits that he hates to be together with Jews. Most of the people who avoid Jewish associations have "good reasons." They are so busy with non-Jewish associations that they "simply don't have time." The boy who prefers "Ethical Culture" or "Christian Science" to Judaism will tell you that he is not running away from things Jewish, but is attracted by the values of the other groups.

In some cases, of course, these "reasons" may actually be the real reasons. Still, there are certain facts which make one wonder. The non-Jewish partner in a mixed marriage will frequently be much more realistic in regard to the education of his children. He seems to see the necessity for the child's growing up with a clear understanding of his being either inside or outside the Jewish group. The Jewish partner often takes the position that children in the United States can grow up simply as human beings. He would deny that he is guided by the same sentiment which has prompted many rich Austrian and German Jews to baptize their children and otherwise to link them as much as possible with typically non-Jewish groups.

However, if the aversion of our atheist for the symbols of Jewish religion were his only motive, he should feel the same aversion against symbols of any organized religion. That this is not the case shows that something else underlies his behavior. The Jewish child from an unorthodox home who tells his mother, "If I see the old Jewish man praying with his *talith*, it makes me feel good; it is as if I pray myself," shows that religious indifference does not necessarily lead to such an aversion. Why does the merchant who refuses to contribute to the Jewish cause spend lavishly on every non-Jewish activity? Why do camps which accommodate only Jewish children hire only non-Jewish counselors and have a Christian Sunday service, but no Jewish songs or other Jewish activities?

SELF-HATRED AS A SOCIAL PHENOMENON

An attempt has been made to explain Jewish self-hatred as the outgrowth of certain deep-seated human instincts. This behavior seems to be a prime example of what Freud calls the drive to self-destruction or the "death instinct." However, an explanation like that is of little value. Why does the Englishman not have the same amount of hatred against his countrymen, or the German against the German, as the Jew against the Jew? If the self-hatred were the result of a general instinct, we should expect its degree to depend only on the personality of the individual. But the amount of self-hatred the individual Jew shows seems to depend far more on his attitude toward Judaism than on his personality.

Jewish self-hatred is a phenomenon which has its parallel in many underprivileged groups. One of the better known and most extreme cases of self-hatred can be found among American Negroes. Negroes distinguish within their group four or five strata according to skin shade—the lighter the skin the higher the strata. This discrimination among themselves goes so far that a girl with a light skin may refuse to marry a man with a darker skin. An element of self-hatred which is less strong but still clearly distinguishable may also be found among the second generation of Greek, Italian, Polish, and other immigrants to this country.

The dynamics of self-hatred and its relation to social facts become apparent by a somewhat closer examination. A Jewish girl at a fashionable Midwestern university confided she had told her friends that her parents were American-born, although actually her father is a first-generation immigrant from the East, speaking with a strong accent. Now she has a bad conscience toward her father, whom she actually loves, and plans to leave the university. Why did she do it? She felt that if her parentage were known, she would not be eligible to certain more fashionable circles on the campus.

The cause of this action against the family group is rather obvious: the individual has certain expectations and goals for the future. Belonging to his group is seen as an impediment to reaching those goals. This leads to a tendency to set himself apart from the group. In the case of the student, this resulted in a conflict with the psychological tie to the family, a conflict which she was unable to stand. However, it is easy to see how such a frustration may lead to a feeling of hatred against one's own group as the source of the frustration.

A Jewish lady, dining in a fashionable restaurant with a non-Jewish friend, was greatly annoyed by a couple of other guests who behaved in a loud manner and were obviously somewhat intoxicated. For one reason or another, she had the feeling that these people might be Jewish. Her friend made a remark which clearly indicated that they were not Jewish. The lady felt greatly relieved, and from that moment on was amused rather than annoyed by their boisterousness. Such incidents are of daily occurrence. The outstanding phenomenon here seems to be an extreme sensitivity in the Jewish woman regarding the behavior of other Jews, similar to the sensitivity of a mother about the behavior of her children when they perform in public. Common to this case and to that of the student is the feeling of the individual that his position is threatened or that his future is endangered through his being identified with a certain group.

The sensitivity in regard to the conduct of other members of a group is but an expression of a fundamental fact of group life, namely, interdependence of fate. It is revealing that Jews who claim to be free of Jewish ties still frequently show a great sensitivity. It indicates that, in spite of their words, these people are somehow aware of the social reality. Indeed, life, freedom, and the pursuit of happiness of every Jewish community in America and every individual American Jew depends in a specific way on the social status which the Jews as a group have in the more inclusive community of the United States. In case Hitler should win the war, this special interdependence of fate will become the most important determining factor in the life of every single Jew. If Hitler should lose, this interdependence will still be one of the dominant factors for the lives of our children.

THE FORCES TOWARD AND AWAY FROM GROUP MEMBERSHIP

Analytically, one can distinguish two types of forces in regard to the member of any group, one type drawing him into the group and keeping him inside, the other driving him away from the group. The sources of the forces toward the group may be manifold: perhaps the individual feels attracted to other members of the group, perhaps the other members draw him in, maybe he is interested in the goal of the group or feels in accord with its ideology, or he may prefer this group to being alone. Similarly, the forces away from the group may be the result of any sort of disagreeable features of the group itself, or they may be an expression of the greater attractiveness of an outside group.

If the balance between the forces toward and away from the group is negative, the individual will leave the group if no other factors intervene. Under "free" conditions, therefore, a group will contain only those members for whom the positive forces are stronger than the negative. If a group is not attractive enough to a sufficient number of individuals, it will disappear.

We must realize, however, that the forces toward and away from the group are not always an expression of the person's own needs. They may be imposed upon the individual by some external power. In other words, an individual may be forced against his will to stay inside a group he would like to leave, or he may be kept outside a group he would like to join. For instance, a dictator closes the borders of the country so that nobody may leave. A fashionable circle keeps many people outside who would like to be included.

COHESIVE AND DISRUPTIVE FORCES IN AN UNDERPRIVILEGED GROUP

An important factor for the strength of the forces toward and away from the group is the degree to which the fulfillment of the individual's own needs is furthered or hampered by his membership in the group. Some groups, like the Chamber of Commerce or the labor union, exist for the express purpose of furthering the interests of their members. On the other hand, membership in any group limits freedom of action for the individual member to some degree. Being married and having a pleasant and efficient wife may be a great help for the husband in achieving his ambitions, but marriage can be a great handicap, too. By and large, one can say that the more the reaching of the individual's goal is furthered or hindered by the group, the more likely it is that the balance of forces toward or away from the group will be positive or negative.

This analysis permits a general statement in regard to members of socially privileged and underprivileged groups. To gain status is one of the outstanding factors determining the behavior of the individual in our society. The privileged group, in addition, usually offers its members more and hinders them less than does the less privileged group. For these reasons, the members of the élite in any country have a strong positive balance in the direction of staying in the élite group. Besides, if an individual wants to leave this élite, he is usually able to do so without hindrance (although there are exceptions).

The member of an underprivileged group is more hampered by his group belongingness. In addition, the tendency to gain status means a force away from such a group. At the same time, we find that in the case of any socially underprivileged group, free mobility across the boundary is limited or entirely prevented by a lack of ability or by external forces. The more privileged majority or an influential section of this majority prohibits free mobility. In every socially underprivileged group, therefore, there are a number of members for whom the balance of the forces toward and away from the group is such that they would prefer to leave it. They are kept inside the group not by their own needs, but by forces which are imposed upon them. This has a far-reaching effect on the atmosphere, structure and organization of every underprivileged group and on the psychology of its members.

GROUP LOYALTY AND NEGATIVE CHAUVINISM

In every group one can distinguish strata which are culturally more central, and others which are more peripheral. The central stratum contains those values, habits, ideas and traditions which are considered most essential and representative for the group. For the musician, this means the ideal musician; for the Englishman, what he considers to be typically English.

People who are loyal to a group have a tendency to rate the more central layers higher. In other words, the average Englishman is "proud" to be English and would dislike being called un-English. Frequently there is a tendency to over-rate the central layer. In such a case we speak of a "100% Americanism" or, more generally, of chauvinism. But a positive rating of the central layers is a logical result of group loyalty and a very essential factor in keeping a group together. Without such loyalty no group can progress and prosper.

Those individuals who would like to leave a group do not have this loyalty. In an underprivileged group, many of these individuals are, nevertheless, forced to stay within the group. As a result, we find in every underprivileged group a number of persons ashamed of their membership. In the case of the Jews, such a Jew will try to move away as far as possible from things Jewish. On his scale of values, he will place those habits, appearances, or attitudes which he considers to be particularly Jewish *not* particularly high; he will rank them low. He will show a "negative chauvinism."

This situation is much aggravated by the following fact: A person for whom the balance is negative will move as far away from the center of Jewish life as the outside majority permits. He will stay on this barrier and be in a constant state of frustration. Actually, he will be more frustrated than those members of the minority who keep psychologically well inside the group. We know from experimental psychology and psychopathology that such frustration leads to an all-around state of high tension with a generalized tendency to aggression. The aggression should, logically, be directed against the majority, which is what hinders the minority member from leaving his group. However, the majority has, in the eyes of these persons, higher status. And besides, the majority is much too powerful to be attacked. Experiments have shown that, under these conditions, aggression is likely to be turned against one's own group or against one's self.

THE POWER OF THE ATTITUDES OF THE PRIVILEGED GROUP

The tendency toward aggression against one's own group, under these circumstances, is strengthened by an additional factor. Mark Twain tells the story of a Negro who was brought up as a white child. When he turns against his mother in a most vicious and cowardly way, his mother says, "That's the nigger in you." In

other words, she has accepted the white man's verdict in characterizing some of the worst features as typical of the Negro.

It is recognized in sociology that the members of the lower
social strata tend to accept the fashions, values, and ideals of the
higher strata. In the case of the underprivileged group it means
that their opinions about themselves are greatly influenced by the
low esteem the majority has for them. This infiltration of the
views and values of what Maurice Pekarsky has called the "gate-
keeper" necessarily heightens the tendency of the Jew with a
negative balance to cut himself loose from things Jewish. The
more typically Jewish people are, or the more typically Jewish
a cultural symbol or behavior pattern is, the more distasteful
they will appear to this person. Being unable to cut himself entirely loose from his Jewish connections and his Jewish past, the
hatred turns upon himself.

ORGANIZATION OF UNDERPRIVILEGED GROUPS

Members of the majority are accustomed to think of a minority
as a homogenous group which they can characterize by a stereotype
like "the Jew" or "the Negro." It has been shown that this stereotype is created in the growing child by the social atmosphere in
which he grows up, and that the degree of prejudice is practically
independent of the amount and kind of actual experience which
the individual has had with members of the minority group.

Actually, *every* group, including every economically or otherwise underprivileged group, contains a number of social strata.
There exists, however, the following difference between the
typical structure of a privileged and an underprivileged group.
The forces acting on an individual member (m) of a privileged
group are directed toward the central layers of that group.
The forces acting on a member of an underprivileged group are
directed away from the central area, toward the periphery of the
group and, if possible, toward the still higher status of the
majority. The member would leave if the barrier set up by the
majority did not prevent him. This picture represents the psychological situation of those members of the underprivileged group

who have a basically negative balance. It is the structure of a group of people who are fundamentally turned against themselves.

It is clear that an effective organization of a group becomes more difficult the more it contains members having a negative balance, and the stronger this negative balance is. It is a well-known fact that the task of organizing a group which is economically or otherwise underprivileged is seriously hampered by those members whose real goal is to leave the group rather than to

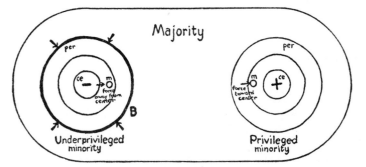

FIGURE XXVI

m, individual member
per, peripheral stratum of group
ce, central stratum of group
B, barrier prohibiting passing

promote it. This deep-seated conflict of goals within an underprivileged group is not always clear to the members themselves. But it is one reason why even a large underprivileged group which would be able to obtain equal rights if it were united for action can be kept rather easily in an inferior position.

LEADERS FROM THE PERIPHERY

It is particularly damaging for the organization and action of a minority group that certain types of leaders are bound to arise in it. In any group, those sections are apt to gain leadership which are more generally successful. In a minority group, individual members who are economically successful, or who have distinguished themselves in their professions, usually gain a higher degree of acceptance by the majority group. This places them culturally on the periphery of the underprivileged group and makes them more likely to be "marginal" persons. They frequently have a negative balance and are particularly eager to have their "good connections" not endangered by too close a contact with those sections of the underprivileged group which are not acceptable to the majority. Nevertheless, they are frequently called for leadership by the underprivileged group because of their status and power. They themselves are usually eager to accept the leading role in the minority, partly as a substitute for gaining status in the majority, partly because such leadership makes it possible for them to have and maintain additional contact with the majority.

As a result, we find the rather paradoxical phenomenon of what one might call "the leader from the periphery." Instead of having a group led by people who are proud of the group, who wish to stay in it and to promote it, we see minority leaders who are lukewarm toward the group, who may, under a thin cover of loyalty, be fundamentally eager to leave the group, or who try to use their power outright for acts of negative chauvinism. Having achieved a relatively satisfactory status among non-Jews, these individuals are chiefly concerned with maintaining the status quo and so try to soft-pedal any action which might arouse the attention of the non-Jew. These Jews would never think of accusing Knudsen of "double loyalty" for presiding at an American Danish rally, but they are so accustomed to viewing Jewish events with eyes of the anti-Semite that they are afraid of the accusation of double loyalty in the case of any outspoken Jewish action. If there is "danger" of a Jew's being appointed to the Supreme Court, they will not hesitate to warn the President against such an action.

As stated in the beginning, it may be difficult to determine in a given case exactly where the boundary between Jewish chauvinism, normal loyalty, and negative chauvinism may lie. However, our analysis should make it clear that an unmanly and unwise (because unrealistic) hush-hush policy springs from the same forces of negative chauvinism or fear as Jewish self-hatred does. In fact, it is one of the most damaging varieties of Jewish self-hatred.

There are indications that the percentage of such people among leading members of the American Jewish community has increased since the First World War. In spite of the disastrous consequences which this policy had for the Jews of Germany, there are probably more Jews in America today who have a negative balance than there were in 1910.

On the other hand, the development of Palestine, the recent history of the European Jews, and the threat of Hitlerism have made the issues more clear. A few Jews, such as the infamous Captain Naumann in Germany, have become Fascistic themselves under the threat of Fascism. However, many Jews who had lost contact with Judaism have come back under the threat of Nazism in Europe. The history of revolutions teaches us that the most active and efficient leadership of the underprivileged has come from certain individuals who left the privileged groups and voluntarily linked their fate with that of the minority. These people must have had, for one reason or another, a particularly strong positive balance of the forces toward and away from the group. It would be in agreement with historical experience if there were found to be efficient leaders among those who have re-entered the ranks of the conscious Jew.

WHAT CAN BE DONE ABOUT JEWISH SELF-HATRED?

Self-hatred seems to be a psychopathological phenomenon, and its prevention may seem mainly a task for the psychiatrist. However, modern psychology knows that many psychological phenomena are but an expression of a social situation in which the individual finds himself. In a few cases, Jewish self-hatred may grow out of a neurotic or otherwise abnormal personality, but in the great majority of cases it is a phenomenon in persons of normal mental health. In other words, it is a social-psychological phenomenon, even though it usually influences deeply the total personality. In fact, neurotic trends in Jews are frequently the result of their lack of adjustment to just such group problems.

Jewish self-hatred will die out only when actual equality of status with the non-Jew is achieved. Only then will the enmity against one's own group decrease to the relatively insignificant proportions characteristic of the majority group's. Sound self-criticism will replace it. This does not mean that nothing can be done meanwhile. After all, we do have a great many Jews who can hardly be classified as anti-Semitic.

The only way to avoid Jewish self-hatred in its various forms is a change of the negative balance between the forces toward and away from the Jewish group into a positive balance, the creation of loyalty to the Jewish group instead of negative chauvinism. We are unable to safeguard our fellow Jews or our growing children today against those handicaps which are the result of their being Jewish. However, we can try to build up a Jewish education both on the children's level and on the adult level to counteract the *feeling of inferiority* and the *feeling of fear* which are the most important sources of the negative balance.

The feeling of inferiority of the Jew is but an indication of the fact that he sees things Jewish with the eyes of the unfriendly majority. I remember how, as an adolescent, I was deeply disturbed by the idea that the accusation against the Jews as being incapable of constructive work might be true. I know that many Jewish adolescents growing up in an atmosphere of prejudice felt similarly. Today, a Jewish youth who has watched Palestine grow is in an infinitely better situation. Whatever one's opinion about Zionism as a political program may be, no one who has observed closely the German Jews during the fateful first weeks after Hitler's rise to power will deny that thousands of German Jews were saved from suicide only by the famous article of the *Jüdische Rundschau*, with its headlines *"Jasagen zum Judentum"* ("Saying Yes to Being a Jew"). The ideas expressed there were the rallying point and the source of strength for Zionist and non-Zionist alike.

To counteract fear and make the individual strong to face whatever the future holds, there is nothing so important as a clear and fully accepted belonging to a group whose fate has a positive meaning. A long-range view which includes the past and the future of Jewish life, and links the solution of the minority problem with the problem of the welfare of all human beings is one of these possible sources of strength. A strong feeling of being part and parcel of the group and having a positive attitude toward it is, for children and adults alike, the sufficient condition for the avoidance of attitudes based on self-hatred.

To build up such feeling of group belongingness on the basis of active responsibility for the fellow Jew should be one of the outstanding policies in Jewish education. That does not mean that we can create in our children a feeling of belongingness by *forcing* them to go to the Sunday School or *Heder*. Such a procedure means the establishment in early childhood of the same pattern of enforced group belongingness which is characteristic of the psychological situation for the negative chauvinists and it is sure to create in the long run exactly this attitude. Too many young Jews have been driven away from Judaism by too much *Heder*. Our children should be brought up in contact with Jewish life in such a way that phrases like "the person looks Jewish" or "acts Jewish" take on a positive rather than a negative tone. That implies that a Jewish religious school should be conducted on a level at least comparable to the pedagogical standards of the rest of our schools.

Organizationally, the group as a whole would probably be greatly strengthened if we could get rid of our negative chauvinists. Such an expulsion is not possible. However, we might be able to approximate more closely a state of affairs in which belonging to the Jewish group is based—at least as far as we ourselves are concerned—on the willingness of the individual to accept active responsibility and sacrifice for the group. In my opinion, Jews have made a great mistake in assuming that to keep a large membership one should demand as little as possible from the individual. Strong groups are not built up that way, but rather by the opposite policy. We could learn something here, for instance, from the

Catholic group. Actually, demanding a spirit of self-sacrifice from the individual is far more likely to decrease self-hatred.

One final point deserves mention. Many Jews seem to believe that prejudice against the Jew would disappear if every individual conducted himself properly—this in spite of all indications that the two facts have but little inter-communication. Jewish parents are accustomed to stress more than do other parents the importance of appearing well in public. This emphasis is one of the origins of the over-sensitivity to the behavior of the fellow Jew that we have mentioned previously, and a source of endless self-consciousness and tension. The more the individual learns to see the Jewish question as a social problem rather than as an individual problem of good conduct, thus placing a double burden on his shoulders, the more he will be able to act normally and freely. Such a normalizing of the tension level is probably the most important condition for the elimination of Jewish-self-hatred.

13

ACTION RESEARCH AND MINORITY PROBLEMS

(1946)

IN THE last year and a half I have had occasion to have contact with a great variety of organizations, institutions, and individuals who came for help in the field of group relations. They included representatives of communities, school systems, single schools, minority organizations of a variety of backgrounds and objectives; they included labor and management representatives, departments of the national and state governments, and so on.

Two basic facts emerged from these contacts: there exists a great amount of good-will, of readiness to face the problem squarely and really to do something about it. If this amount of serious good-will could be transformed into organized, efficient action, there would be no danger for inter-group relations in the United States. But exactly here lies the difficulty. These eager people feel themselves to be in the fog. They feel in the fog on three counts: 1. What is the present situation? 2. What are the dangers? 3. And most important of all, what shall we do?

We have been conducting an interview survey among workers in inter-group relations in the State of Connecticut. We wanted to know their line of thinking, their line of action, and the major barriers which they encounter. Not a few of those whose very job is the improvement of inter-group relations state that perhaps the greatest obstacle to their work is their own lack of clarity of what ought to be done. How is economic and social discrimination to be attacked if we think not in terms of generalities but in terms of the inhabitants of that particular main street and those side and end streets which make up that small or large town in which the individual group worker is supposed to do his job?

One of the consequences of this unclearness is the lack of standards by which to measure progress. When the inter-group worker, coming home from the good-will meeting which he helped to instigate, thinks of the dignitaries he was able to line up, the stirring appeals he heard, the impressive setting of the stage, and the good quality of the food, he cannot help feeling elated by the general atmosphere and the words of praise from his friends all around. Still, a few days later, when the next case of discrimination becomes known he often wonders whether all this was more than a white-wash and whether he is right in accepting the acknowledgment of his friends as a measuring stick for the progress of his work.

This lack of objective standards of achievement has two severe effects:

1. It deprives the workers in inter-group relations of their legitimate desire for satisfaction on a realistic basis. Under these circumstances, satisfaction or dissatisfaction with his own achievement becomes mainly a question of temperament.

2. In a field that lacks objective standards of achievement, no learning can take place. If we cannot judge whether an action has led forward or backward, if we have no criteria for evaluating the relation between effort and achievement, there is nothing to prevent us from making the wrong conclusions and to encourage the wrong work habits. Realistic fact-finding and evaluation is a prerequisite for any learning. Social research should be one of the top priorities for the practical job of improving inter-group relations.

CHARACTER AND FUNCTION OF RESEARCH FOR THE PRACTICE
OF INTER-GROUP RELATIONS

The research needed for social practice can best be characterized as research for social management or social engineering. It is a type of action-research, a comparative research on the conditions and effects of various forms of social action, and research leading to social action. Research that produces nothing but books will not suffice.

This by no means implies that the research needed is in any respect less scientific or "lower" than what would be required for pure science in the field of social events. I am inclined to hold the opposite to be true. Institutions interested in engineering, such as the Massachusetts Institute of Technology, have turned more and more to what is called basic research. In regard to social engineering, too, progress will depend largely on the rate with which basic research in social sciences can develop deeper insight into the laws which govern social life. This "basic social research" will have to include mathematical and conceptual problems of theoretical analysis. It will have to include the whole range of descriptive fact-finding in regard to small and large social bodies. Above all, it will have to include laboratory and field experiments in social change.

INTEGRATING SOCIAL SCIENCES

An attempt to improve inter-group relations has to face a wide variety of tasks. It deals with problems of attitude and stereotypes in regard to other groups and to one's own group, with problems of development of attitudes and conduct during childhood and adolescence, with problems of housing, and the change of the legal structure of the community; it deals with problems of status and caste, with problems of economic discrimination, with political leadership, and with leadership in many aspects of community life. It deals with the small social body of a family, a club or a friendship group, with the larger social body of a school or a school system, with neighborhoods and with social bodies of the size of a community, of the state, a nation and with international problems.

We are beginning to see that it is hopeless to attack any one of these aspects of inter-group relations without considering the others. This holds equally for the practical and the scientific sides of the question. Psychology, sociology, and cultural anthropology each have begun to realize that without the help of the other neither will be able to proceed very far. During the last five years first timidly, now very clearly, a desire for an integrated approach has become articulated. What this integration would mean specifically is still open. It may mean an amalgamation of the social sciences into one social science. It may mean, on the other hand, merely the co-operation of various sciences for the practical objective of improving social management. However, the next decade will doubtless witness serious attempts of an integrated approach to social research. I am of the opinion that economics will have to be included in this symphony if we are to understand and to handle inter-group relations more effectively.

TWO TYPES OF RESEARCH OBJECTIVES

It is important to understand clearly that social research concerns itself with two rather different types of questions, namely the study of general laws of group life and the diagnosis of a specific situation.

Problems of general laws deal with the relation between possible conditions and possible results. They are expressed in "if so" propositions. The knowledge of laws can serve as guidance for the achievement of certain objectives under certain conditions. To act correctly, it does not suffice, however, if the engineer or the surgeon knows the general laws of physics or physiology. He has to know too the specific character of the situation at hand. This character is determined by a scientific fact-finding called diagnosis. For any field of action both types of scientific research are needed.

Until recently, fact-finding on inter-group relations has been largely dominated by surveys. We have become somewhat critical of these surveys of inter-group relations. Although they are potentially important, they have, as a rule, used rather superficial methods of poll taking and not the deeper searching of the interview type used by Likert which gives us some insight into the motivations behind the sentiments expressed.

The second cause of dissatisfaction is the growing realization that mere diagnosis—and surveys are a type of diagnosis—does not suffice. In inter-group relations as in other fields of social management the diagnosis has to be complemented by experimental comparative studies of the effectiveness of various techniques of change.

THE FUNCTION AND POSITION OF RESEARCH WITHIN SOCIAL PLANNING AND ACTION

At least of equal importance to the content of the research on inter-group relations is its proper placement within social life. When, where, and by whom should social research be done?

Since we are here interested in social management let us examine somewhat more closely the process of planning.

Planning starts usually with something like a general idea. For one reason or another it seems desirable to reach a certain objective. Exactly how to circumscribe this objective, and how to reach it, is frequently not too clear. The first step then is to examine the idea carefully in the light of the means available. Frequently more fact-finding about the situation is required. If this first period of planning is successful, two items emerge: namely, an "overall plan" of how to reach the objective and secondly, a decision in regard to the first step of action. Usually this planning has also somewhat modified the original idea.

The next period is devoted to executing the first step of the overall plan.

In highly developed fields of social management, such as modern factory management or the execution of a war, this second step is followed by certain fact-findings. For example, in the bombing of Germany a certain factory may have been chosen as the first target after careful consideration of various priorities and of the best means and ways of dealing with this target. The attack is pressed home and immediately a reconnaissance plane follows with the one objective of determining as accurately and objectively as possible the new situation.

This reconnaissance or fact-finding has four functions. First it should evaluate the action. It shows whether what has been achieved is above or below expectation. Secondly, it gives the planners a chance to learn, that is, to gather new general insight, for instance, regarding the strength and weakness of certain weapons or techniques of action. Thirdly, this fact-finding should serve as a basis for correctly planning the next step. Finally, it serves as a basis for modifying the "over-all plan."

The next step again is composed of a circle of planning, executing, and reconnaissance or fact-finding for the purpose of evaluating the results of the second step, for preparing the rational basis for planning the third step, and for perhaps modifying again the overall plan.

Rational social management, therefore, proceeds in a spiral of steps each of which is composed of a circle of planning, action, and fact-finding about the result of the action.

With this in mind, let us examine for a moment the way inter-group relations are handled. I cannot help feeling that the person returning from a successful completion of a good-will meeting is like the captain of a boat who somehow has felt that his ship steers too much to the right and therefore has turned the steering wheel sharply to the left. Certain signals assure him that the rudder has followed the move of the steering wheel. Happily he goes to dinner. In the meantime, of course, the boat moves in circles. In the field of inter-group relations all too frequently action is based on observations made "within the boat" and too seldom based on objective criteria in regard to the relations of the movement of the boat to the objective to be reached.

We need reconnaisance to show us whether we move in the right direction and with what speed we move. Socially, it does not suffice that university organizations produce new scientific insight. It will be necessary to install fact-finding procedures, social eyes and ears, right into social action bodies.

The idea of research or fact-finding branches of agencies devoted to improving inter-group relations is not new. However, some of them did little more than collect newspaper clippings. The last few years have seen a number of very significant developments. About two years ago the American Jewish Congress established the Commission on Community Interrelations. This is an action-research organization designed primarily to function as a service organization to Jewish and non-Jewish bodies in the field of group interrelations. It is mainly interested in the group approach as compared to the individual approach on the one hand and the mass approach by way of radio and newspaper on the other. These latter two important lines are the focus of attention of the research unit of the American Jewish Committee.

Various programs try to make use of our educational system for betterment of inter-group relations, such as that of the American Council on Education, the College Study in Inter-group Relations at teachers colleges, the Citizenship Education Study in Detroit, and, in a more overall way, the Bureau for Intercultural Education. They all show an increased sensitivity for a more realistic, that is, more scientific, procedure of evaluation and self-evaluation. The same holds in various degrees for undertakings specifically devoted to Negro-White relations, such as the American Council on Race Relations in Chicago, the Urban League, and others. It is significant that the State Commission Against Discrimination in the State of New York has a subcommittee for co-operation with research projects and that the Inter-Racial Commission of the State of Connecticut is actively engaged in research. The recent creation of major research institutions at universities has also helped to broaden the vistas of many of the existing action organizations, making them more confident of the possibilities of using scientific techniques for their purposes.

I cannot possibly attempt even in the form of a survey to discuss the many projects and findings which are emerging from these research undertakings. They include surveys of the methods which have been used until now, such as reported in *Action for Unity;*[1] studies of the development of attitudes in children; studies of the relation between inter-group attitudes and such factors as political belief, position in one's own group; experiments about how best to react in case of a verbal attack along prejudice lines; change experiments with criminal gangs and with com-

[1] Goodwin Watson, *Action for Unity.* New York, Harper and Brothers, (1946).

munities; the development of many new diagnostic tests; and last but not least, the development of more precise theories of social change. Not too many of the results of these projects have yet found their way into print. However, I am confident that the next few years will witness rapidly increased output of significant and practical studies.

EXAMPLE OF A CHANGE EXPERIMENT ON MINORITY PROBLEMS

One example may illustrate the potentialities of co-operation between practitioners and social scientists. In the beginning of this year the Chairman of the Advisory Committee on Race Relations for the State of Connecticut, who is at the same time a leading member of the Interracial Commission of the State of Connecticut, approached us with a request to conduct a workshop for fifty community workers in the field of intergroup relations from all over the state of Connecticut.

A project emerged in which three agencies co-operated, the Advisory Committee on Intergroup Relations of the State of Connecticut, The Commission on Community Interrelations of the American Jewish Congress, and the Research Center for Group Dynamics at the Massachusetts Institute of Technology. The State Advisory Committee is composed of members of the Interracial Commission of the State of Connecticut, a member of the State Department of Education of the State of Connecticut, and the person in charge of the Connecticut Valley Region of the Conference of Christians and Jews. The state of Connecticut seems to be unique in having an interracial commission as a part of its regular government. It was apparent that any improvement of techniques which could be linked with this strategic central body would have a much better chance of a wide-spread and lasting effect. After a thorough discussion of various possibilities the following change-experiment was designed co-operatively.

Recent research findings have indicated that the ideologies and stereotypes which govern inter-group relations should not be viewed as individual character traits but that they are anchored in cultural standards, that their stability and their change depend largely on happenings in groups as groups. Experience with leadership training had convinced us that the workshop setting is among the most powerful tools for bringing about improvement of skill in handling inter-group relations.

Even a good and successful workshop, however, seems seldom to have the chance to lead to long-range improvements in the field of inter-group relations. The individual who comes home from the workshop full of enthusiasm and new insights will again have to face the community, one against perhaps 100,000. Obviously, the chances are high that his success will not be up to his new level of aspiration, and that soon disappointments will set him back again. We are facing here a question which is of prime importance for any social change, namely the problem of its permanence.

To test certain hypotheses in regard to the effect of individual as against group settings, the following variations were introduced into the experimental workshop. Part of the delegates came as usual, one individual from a town. For a number of communities, however, it was decided the attempt would be made to secure a number of delegates and if possible to develop in the workshop teams who would keep up their team relationship after the workshop. This should give a greater chance for permanency of the enthusiasm and group productivity and should also multiply the power of the participants to bring about the desired change. A third group of delegates to the workshop would receive a certain amount of expert help even after they returned to the community.

The first step in carrying out such a design calls for broad fact-finding about the different types of inter-group problems which the various communities have to face. Communities and teams of group workers in the communities would have to be selected so that the results of the three variations would be possible to compare. In other words, this project had to face the same problems which we mention as typical for the planning process in general.

The experiences of the members of the State Advisory Board of the Interracial Commission of the State of Connecticut were able quickly to provide sufficient data to determine the towns which should be studied more accurately. To evaluate the effect of the workshop a diagnosis before the workshop would have to be carried out to determine, among other things, the line of thinking of the community workers, their main line of action and the main barriers they have to face. A similar re-diagnosis would have to be carried out some months after the workshop.

To understand why the workshop produced whatever change or lack of change would be found, it is obviously necessary to record scientifically the essential happenings during the workshop. Here, I feel, research faces its most difficult task. To record the content of the lecture or the program would by no means suffice. Description of the form of leadership has to take into account the amount of initiative shown by individuals and subgroups, the division of the trainees into subgroups, the frictions within and between these subgroups, the crises and their outcome, and, above all, the total management pattern as it changes from day to day. These large-scale aspects, more than anything else, seem to determine what a workshop will accomplish. The task which social scientists have to face in objectively recording these data is not too different from that of the historian. We will have to learn to handle these relatively large units of periods and social bodies without lowering the standards of validity and reliability to which we are accustomed in the psychological recording of the more microscopic units of action and periods of minutes or seconds of activity.

The methods of recording the essential events of the workshop included an evaluation session at the end of every day. Observers who had attended the various subgroup sessions reported (into a recording machine) the leadership pattern they had observed, the progress or lack of progress in the development of the groups from a conglomeration of individuals to an integrated "we" and so on. The group leaders gave their view of the same sessions and a number of trainees added their comments.

I have been deeply impressed with the tremendous pedagogical effect which these evaluation meetings, designed for the purpose of scientific recording, had on the training process. The atmos-

phere of objectivity, the readiness by the faculty to discuss openly
their mistakes, far from endangering their position, seemed to lead
to an enhancement of appreciation and to bring about that mood
of relaxed objectivity which is nowhere more difficult to achieve
than in the field of inter-group relations which is loaded with
emotionality and attitude rigidity even among the so-called liberals
and those whose job it is to promote inter-group relations.

This and similar experiences have convinced me that we should
consider action, research, and training as a triangle that should
be kept together for the sake of any of its corners. It is seldom
possible to improve the action pattern without training personnel.
In fact today the lack of competent training personnel is one of
the greatest hindrances to progress in setting up more experimentation. The training of large numbers of social scientists who can
handle scientific problems but are also equipped for the delicate
task of building productive, hard-hitting teams with practitioners
is a prerequisite for progress in social science as well as in
social management for intergroup relations.

As I watched, during the workshop, the delegates from different
towns all over Connecticut transform from a multitude of unrelated
individuals, frequently opposed in their outlook and their interests, into co-operative teams not on the basis of sweetness but
on the basis of readiness to face difficulties realistically, to apply
honest fact-finding, and to work together to overcome them; when
I saw the pattern of role-playing emerge, saw the major responsibilities move slowly according to plan from the faculty to the
trainees; when I saw, in the final session, the State Advisory
Committee receive the backing of the delegates for a plan of linking the teachers colleges throughout the state with certain aspects
of group relations within the communities; when I heard the
delegates and teams of delegates from various towns present their
plans for city workshops and a number of other projects to go
into realization immediately, I could not help feeling that the
close integration of action, training, and research holds tremendous
possibilities for the field of inter-group relations. I would like to
pass on this feeling to you.

Inter-group relations are doubtless one of the most crucial

aspects on the national and international scene. We know today better than ever before that they are potentially dynamite. The strategy of social research must take into account the dangers involved.

We might distinguish outside adversities and barriers to social science and the inner dangers of research procedures. Among the first we find a group of people who seem to subscribe to the idea that we do not need more social science. Among these admirers of common sense we find practitioners of all types, politicians and college presidents. Unfortunately there are a good number of physical scientists among those who are against a vigorous promotion of the social sciences. They seem to feel that the social sciences have not produced something of real value for the practice of social management and therefore will never do so. I guess there is no other way to convince these people than by producing better social science.

A second threat to social science comes from "groups in power." These people can be found in management on any level, among labor leaders, among politicians, some branches of the government, and among members of Congress. Somehow or other they all seem to be possessed by the fear that they could not do what they want to do if they, and others, really knew the facts. I think social scientists should be careful to distinguish between the legitimate and not legitimate elements behind this fear. For instance, it would be most unhealthy if the findings of the Gallup Poll were automatically to determine policy for what should and should not become law in the United States. We will have to recognize the difference between fact-finding and policy setting and to study carefully the procedures by which fact-finding should be fed into the social machinery of legislation to produce a democratic effect.

Doubtless, however, a good deal of unwillingness to face reality lies behind the enmity to social research of some of the people in power positions.

A third type of very real anxiety on the part of practitioners can be illustrated by the following example. Members of community councils to whom I have had the occasion to report results of research on group interrelations reacted with the feeling that the social scientists at the university or in the research arm of some national organization would sooner or later be in the position to tell the local community workers all over the states exactly what to do and what not to do.

They obviously envisaged a social science "technocracy." This fear seems to be a very common misunderstanding based on the term "law." The community workers failed to realize that lawfulness in social as in physical science means an "if so" relation, a linkage between hypothetical conditions and hypothetical effects. These laws do *not* tell *what* conditions exist locally, at a given place at a given time. In other words, the laws don't do the job of diagnosis which has to be done locally. Neither do laws prescribe the strategy for change. In social management, as in medicine, the practitioner will usually have the choice between various methods of treatment and he will require as much skill and ingenuity as the physician in regard to both diagnosis and treatment.

It seems to be crucial for the progress of social science that the practitioner understand that through social sciences and only through them he can hope to gain the power necessary to do a good job. Unfortunately there is nothing in social laws and social research which will force the practitioner toward the good. Science gives more freedom and power to both the doctor and the murderer, to democracy and Fascism. The social scientist should recognize his responsibility also in respect to this.

RESEARCH ON MAJORITIES AND MINORITIES

It has not been the intention of this paper to discuss detailed findings of social research in inter-group relations. I feel, however, that I should mention two points which illustrate, I think, basic aspects.

Inter-group relations is a two-way affair. This means that to improve relations between groups both of the interacting groups have to be studied.

In recent years we have started to realize that so-called minority problems are in fact majority problems, that the Negro problem is the problem of the white, that the Jewish problem is the problem of the non-Jew, and so on. It is also true of course that intergroup relations cannot be solved without altering certain aspects of conduct and sentiment of the minority group. One of the most severe obstacles in the way of improvement seems to be the notorious lack of confidence and self-esteem of most minority groups. Minority groups tend to accept the implicit judgment of those who have status even where the judgment is directed against themselves. There are many forces which tend to develop in the children, adolescents, and adults of minorities deep-seated antagonism to their own group. An over-degree of submissiveness, guilt, emotionality, and other causes and forms of ineffective behavior follows. Neither an individual nor a group that is at odds with itself can live normally or live happily with other groups.

It should be clear to the social scientist that it is hopeless to cope with this problem by providing sufficient self-esteem for members of minority groups as individuals. The discrimination which these individuals experience is not directed against them as individuals but as group members and only by raising their self-esteem as group members to the normal level can a remedy be produced.

Many whites in the South seem to realize that one prerequisite for progress is the enhancement of self-esteem of the southern Negro. On the other hand, the idea of a positive program of increasing group loyalties seems to be paradoxical to many liberals. We seem to have become accustomed to linking the question of group loyalty and group self-esteem with jingoism.

The solution, I think, can be found only through a development which would bring the general level of group esteem and group loyalty which in themselves are perfectly natural and necessary phenomena to the same level for all groups of society. That means every effort should be made to lower the inflated self-esteem of the 100 percenters. They should learn the prayer from the musical-play, *Oklahoma*. "Dear God, make me see that I am not better than my fellow men." However it is essential to learn the second half of this prayer that goes something like "but that I am every darn bit as good as he." From the experiences thus far I would judge that raising the self-esteem of the minority groups is one of the most strategic means for the improvement of inter-group relations.

The last point I would like to mention concerns the relation between the local, the national, and the international scenes. No one working in the field of inter-group relations can be blind to the fact that we live today in one world. Whether it will become politically one world or two worlds, there is no doubt that so far as interdependence of events is concerned we are living in one world. Whether we think of the Catholics, or the Jews, the Greeks, or the Negroes every group within the United States is deeply affected by happenings in other places on the globe. Inter-group relations in this country will be formed to a large degree by the events on the internationl scene and particularly by the fate of the colonial peoples. It will be crucial whether or not the policy of this country will follow what Raymond Kennedy has called the international Jim Crow policy of the colonial empires. Are we ready to give up the policy followed in the Philippines and to regress when dealing with the United States' dependencies to that policy of exploitation which has made colonial imperialism the most hated institution the world over? Or will we follow the philosophy which John Collier has developed in regard to the American Indians and which the Institute of Ethnic Affairs is proposing for the American dependencies? This is a pattern which leads gradually to independence, equality, and co-operation. Whatever the effect of a policy of permanent exploitation would be on the international scene, it could not help having a deep effect on the situation within the United States. Jim Crowism on the international scene will hamper tremendously progress of inter-group relations within the United States and is likely to endanger every aspect of democracy.

The development of inter-group relations is doubtless full of danger and the development of social science in this field faces many obstacles. The picture, however, which I have been able to paint, of the progress of research and particularly of the progress that the organization of social research has made during the last few years, makes me feel that we have learned much. A large scale effort of social research on inter-group relations doubtless would be able to have a lasting effect on the history of this country.

It is equally clear, however, that this job demands from the social scientists an utmost amount of courage. It needs courage as Plato defines it: "Wisdom concerning dangers." It needs the best of what the best among us can give, and the help of everybody.

SUGGESTED READINGS

Allport, G. "Catharsis and the Reduction of Prejudice." *Journal of Social Issues*, (1945), I, No. 3.
—— "Psychology of Participation." *Psychological Review*, (1945), 53, 117–132.
Bales, R. F. "Social Therapy for a Social Disorder—Compulsive Drinking." *Journal of Social Issues*, (1945), I, No. 3.
Barker, R., Dembo, T., and Lewin, K. "Frustration and Regression: An Experiment with Young Children." *Studies in Topological and Vector Psychology II. University of Iowa Studies: Studies in Child Welfare*, (1941), XVIII, No. 2.
Bavelas, A. "Morale and the Training of Leadership," in *Civilian Morale*, Second Yearbook of the Society for the Psychological Study of Social Issues. Boston: Houghton Mifflin, (1942).
Bavelas, A. and Lewin, K. "Training in Democratic Leadership." *Journal of Abnormal and Social Psychology*, (1942), 37, 115–119.
Boring, E. G. *The Physical Dimensions of Consciousness*. D. Appleton-Century Co. Inc., (1933).
Brandeis, L. D. "A Call to the Educated Jew." *Menorah Journal*, (1915), I, 1.
Bridgman, P. W. *The Logic of Modern Physics*. Macmillan & Co., (1927).
Brown, J. F. *Psychology and the Social Order*. New York: McGraw-Hill Publishing Co. Inc., (1936).
—— "Towards a Theory of Social Dynamics." *Journal of Social Psychology*, (1935), VI, 182–213.
Burgess, E. W. and Cottrell, L. S. *Predicting Success and Failure in Marriage*. New York: Prentice-Hall, (1939).
Cartwright, D. "Public Opinion Polls and Democratic Leadership." *Journal of Social Issues*, (1946), II, No. 2, 23–32.
Cartwright, D. and Festinger, L. "A Quantitative Theory of Decision." *Psychological Review*, (1943), 50, 595.
Farago, L., ed. *German Psychological Warfare: Survey and Bibliography*. New York: Committee for National Morale, (1941).

Farber, M. L. "Suffering and Time Perspective of the Prisoner." *University of Iowa Studies: Studies in Child Welfare*, (1944), XX, 155–227.

Festinger, L. "Wish, Expectation, and Group Standards as Factors Influencing the Level of Aspiration." *Journal of Abnormal and Social Psychology*, (1942), 37, 184–200.

Frank, L. K. "Time Perspectives." *Journal of Social Philosophy*, (1939), 4, 293–312.

French, J. R. P., Jr. "Disruption and Cohesion of Groups." *Journal of Abnormal and Social Psychology*, (1941), 36, 361–378.

Hall, O. M. "Attitudes and Unemployment: A Comparison of the Opinions and Attitudes of Employed and Unemployed Men." New York, *Archives of Psychology*, (1934), No. 165.

Hamilton, G. V. *A Research in Marriage*. New York: Boni, (1929).

Haydon, E. M. "Re-education and Delinquency." *Journal of Social Issues*, (1945), I, No. 3.

Hendry, C. E., Lippitt, R., and Hogrefe, R. *Camp as a Laboratory for Scoutmaster Training*. New York: Boy Scouts of America, Research and Statistical Service.

Horowitz, E. L. "The Development of Attitudes toward the Negro." *Archives of Psychology*, (1936), No. 194.

Howard, P. and Lippitt, R. "Training Community Leadership toward More Effective Group Living." *Adult Education Bulletin*, August, (1946).

Johnson, W. "The Role of Evaluation in Stuttering Behavior." *Journal of Speech Disorders*, (1938), 3, 85.

Keister, M. E. "The Behavior of Young Children in Failure: An Experimental Attempt to Discover and to Modify Undesirable Responses of Preschool Children to Failure." *Studies in Preschool Education I. University of Iowa Studies: Studies in Child Welfare*, (1937), XIV, 29–84.

Koffka, K. *Principles of Gestalt Psychology*. Kegan Paul & Co, (1935).

Korsch-Escalona, S. "The Effect of Success and Failure upon the Level of Aspiration and Behavior in Manic-Depressive Psychoses." *University of Iowa Studies: Studies in Child Welfare*, (1940), XVI, No. 3, 199–303.

Lasswell, H. D. *Encyclopedia of the Social Sciences*, vol. 9. New York: Macmillan, (1933).

Lewin, K. *The Conceptual Representation and the Measurement of Psychological Forces*. Cambridge University Press, (1938).

Lewin, K. "Constructs in Psychology and Psychological Ecology." *Studies in Topological and Vector Psychology III. University of Iowa Studies: Studies in Child Welfare,* (1944), XX, 1–30.

—— *A Dynamic Theory of Personality.* McGraw-Hill Publishing Co. Inc., (1935).

—— "Environmental Forces," in *A Handbook of Child Psychology,* ed. C. Murchison, Oxford University Press, (1933).

—— "Field Theory and Experiment in Social Psychology: Concepts and Methods." *American Journal of Social Psychology,* (1939), 44, 873–884.

—— *Principles of Topological Psychology.* McGraw-Hill Publishing Co. Inc., (1936).

Lewin, K., Lippitt, R., and White, R. "Patterns of Aggressive Behavior in Experimentally Created 'Social Climates'." *Journal of Social Psychology,* (1939), X, 271–299.

Lippitt, R. "Field Theory and Experiment in Social Psychology: Autocratic and Democratic Group Atmospheres." *American Journal of Sociology,* (1939), 45, 26–49.

—— "Studies on Experimentally Created Autocratic and Democratic Groups." *University of Iowa Studies: Studies in Child Welfare,* 1940, XVI, No. 3, 45–198.

Lippitt, R. and Hendry, C. E. "The Practicality of Democracy," in *Human Nature and Enduring Peace,* Third Yearbook of the Society for the Psychological Study of Social Issues. New York: Reynal and Hitchcock, (1945).

Lippitt, R(osemary). *Camp Fire Girls Program Study,* Part I. New York: Camp Fire Girls, Inc.

Marrow, A. J. and French, J. R. P., Jr. "Changing a Stereotype in Industry." *Journal of Social Issues,* (1945), I, No. 3.

Meyers, C. E. "The Effect of Conflicting Authority on the Child." *Studies in Topological and Vector Psychology III. University of Iowa Studies: Studies in Child Welfare,* (1944), XX, 31–98.

Roethlisberger, F. J. *Management and Morale.* Oxford University Press, (1941).

Roethlisberger, F. J. and Dickson, W. J. *Management and the Worker.* Oxford University Press, 1940.

Rogers, C. *Counseling and Psychotherapy.* Boston: Houghton Mifflin, 1942.

Samelson, B. "Does Education Diminish Prejudice?" *Journal of Social Issues,* (1945), I, No. 3.

Sears, P. S. "Level of Aspiration in Academically Successful and Unsuccessful Children." *Journal of Abnormal and Social Psychology,* (1940), 35, 498–536.

Terman, L. M. *Psychological Factors in Marital Happiness.* McGraw-Hill Book Co., (1938).

Watson, G. *Action for Unity.* Harper & Bros., (1947).

Wellman, B. L. "Our Changing Concept of Intelligence." *Journal of Consulting Psychology,* (1938), 2, 97–107.

INDEX

Ability, lack of, 5
Abnormality, 57
Acceptance of new values: belongingness and, 67-68; establishment of, 66-68; freedom of; 65-66; of group goals, 116-18; hostility to, 64-65
Accessibility: difference in, 21-22; regions of, 21-23, 31; in social distance, 20-21
Acculturation, 59
Action. *See* Motoric action
Action for Unity, 207
Action ideology, 64
Action interview, 129
Action research: example of, 208-13; function of, 202-3, 205-8; integration of, 203-4; on minorities and majorities, 213-16; objectives, 204-5
Adequate visual image, 57
Adolescent, eternal, 182, 185
Adolescent, German, 41-42
Advisory Committee on Race Relations, 208, 209-10, 211
Age levels, German, 52-53
Allegiance. *See* Double loyalty
American Council on Education, 207
American Council on Race Relations, 207
American Jewish Committee, 207

American Jewish Congress, 206
Anthropology, cultural 35, 203-4
Anti-Semitism: basis of, 161-62, 182; and belongingness, 176; and children, 170-72, 183; and part-Jews, 177-78; and self-hatred, 198
Ascendant actions, 76-77
Aspiration. *See* Level of aspiration
Assimilation, in Jews: defined, 149; impossibility of, 164, 180
Atmosphere, general cultural, 4
Attitude, 3
Attraction. *See* Valence
Autocracy: changing of to democracy, 49-55; culture of, 48-55; experiments in, 75-83; imposition of, 38-39, 87; morale in, 122-23

Background: influence of, on education, 4; instability of, 146; and perception, 145
Balance, negative, 194-95, 196, 197
Barriers: of bachelor, 95-96; in Ghetto 149-51; in marriage, 95-96; outer, 89; in prewar Germany, 151-55
Basic research, 203